Dan
CARTER

Dan
CARTER

Skills and Performance

with Ron Palenski

Hodder Moa

National Library of New Zealand Cataloguing-in-Publication Data

Dan Carter : skills and performance / Dan Carter with Ron Palenski.

ISBN-13: 978-1-86971-077-4

ISBN-10: 1-86971-077-0

1. Carter, Dan, 1982- 2. Rugby Union football players—New Zealand. 3. Rugby Union football. I. Palenski, Ron. II. Title.

796.333092—dc 22

A Hodder Moa Book

Published in 2006 by Hachette Livre NZ Ltd

4 Whetu Place, Mairangi Bay

Auckland, New Zealand

Designed and produced by Hachette Livre NZ Ltd

Printed by Tien Wah Press Ltd, Singapore

Double page spreads and preliminary pages captions

Page 5: All Blacks v Australia, Jade Stadium, 2006; pages 8–9: All Blacks v Wales, Millennium Stadium, 2005; pages 12–13: All Blacks v Wales, Millennium Stadium, 2005; pages 18–19: All Blacks v England, Twickenham, 2005; pages 36–37: All Blacks v Fiji, North Harbour Stadium, 2005; page 41: All Blacks v England, Twickenham, 2005; pages 46–47: All Blacks v England, Twickenham, 2005; pages 56–57: Canterbury v East Coast, Jade Stadium, 2002; pages 72–73: All Blacks v Wales, Waikato Stadium, 2003; pages 90–91: Crusaders v Stormers, Jade Stadium, 2004; pages 118–119: All Blacks v British and Irish Lions, Westpac Stadium, 2005; pages 148–149: All Blacks v Argentina, Velez Sarsfield Stadium, 2006; pages 164–165: Signing autographs, Basin Reserve, 2005.

To my family — Mum, Dad and Sarah —
and to my fans for their ongoing support.

Acknowledgements

The author, writer and publishers wish to thank the following organisations and people for their assistance with this book: GSM (Dean Hegan, Lou Thompson and Warren Alcock), adidas, the New Zealand Rugby Union, Pacific Brands, Andrew Cornaga (Photosport), Simon Baker (Pro Sport Photos), Marc Weakley, Arran Birchenough (Getty Images), Jo Caird, *North & South*/Jane Wyles, Harvey Cameron Advertising Ltd, Standish & Preece, Christchurch Boys' High School, Ellesmere College.

Contents

Dan Carter
— an Appreciation

In the 1970s when Wales had Barry John and Phil Bennett and a seemingly limitless supply of wizardry in the No 10 jersey, the bard of Welsh rugby, Max Boyce, wrote a song about what he called the Flyhalf Factory. The gist of it was that deep in the valleys somewhere there was a production line that churned out these little chaps who could kick magically with either foot, who could pass off either hand and with sleight of foot could mesmerise the most determined of defenders. Alas for Wales, the factory shut up shop and reopened for business in New Zealand. Or so it seemed.

One of the myths of New Zealand rugby — a myth spread not so much by New Zealanders but by those other nationalities who envy the record of the All Blacks and would dearly love to beat them more often, or even just once — is that the New Zealand game has always been based on hard, rugged forwards and a first five-eighth who kicks the ball out and thus gives his forwards another crack. Ten-man rugby. There have been times when the myth was the reality but more often than not, it's remained myth.

New Zealand have had men in the No 10 jersey on whose backs Max Boyce would have loved to have imprinted, 'Made In Wales'. We can reach back into the mists of time for the names of All Blacks who would have graced any era, but we can stay in the bright sunshine to pinpoint some of the best.

Grant Fox, for example, was first an All Black in 1985 and when he retired — prematurely, some believe — in 1993, there were public laments that we would never see his like again. There were comments that his record number of points for New Zealand surely would never be matched, but the measure of Fox was not merely the points he scored. There was much more to him than that.

Barely had Fox stepped away from the international stage than another came to take his place. Andrew Mehrtens played his first test within two years of Fox playing his last and the anguish of Fox's passing seemed not so keenly felt any more. No disrespect to Fox of course; it just showed the production line was well oiled. It seemed only a historical twinkling of an eye before Mehrtens surpassed Fox's points for New Zealand but, again, it was not the points which were the yardstick. It was the complete first five-eighth game that first Fox and then Mehrtens

When in Rome. Getting a pass away during the 59–10 win against Italy in 2004.

brought with them. Not that Mehrtens had things all his own way. It's still fresh in the memory of New Zealand rugby fans that at times Carlos Spencer was preferred in the black jersey to Mehrtens — a different type of player to Mehrtens, to be sure, but each a footballing genius in his own right.

As Mehrtens and Spencer wound down their New Zealand careers and looked at the retirement home for international players in Britain, there was already a new light dawning in the Canterbury sky.

Only those close to Canterbury rugby would have known much about Dan Carter when he played for New Zealand Under-21 in South Africa, then in the NPC team. It was only when he made the Crusaders for the 2003 Super 12 that the wider rugby public could see that here was, to say the least, a worthy successor. The All Blacks coach at the time, John Mitchell, who was assisted by the Crusaders coach, Robbie Deans, certainly saw the latent value in Carter and took him into the All Blacks. Carter must have had to pinch himself to make sure what was happening to him was real.

Carter made his mark initially at second five-eighth but with the canny Wayne Smith, himself a product of the assembly line, again becoming involved with the All Blacks it seemed evident that the No 10 jersey was destined for Carter. And so it proved.

There have been people close to the All Blacks who have said that Carter is one of the most naturally gifted players they have ever seen. That may be so. But Carter is not, and never was, one to rely on gifts, however natural they may be. For didn't he practise, practise and practise yet again to be able to kick with his right foot almost as competently as he does naturally with his left? And doesn't he kick, kick and kick yet again to ensure the timing is perfect even though he seems the model kicker? It's a hallmark of great players that they do things so well, and so repetitively well, that it just seems natural. Behind every natural talent is a power of work and dedication.

Carter is a dedicated worker and though he hasn't yet played 100 first-class games, there can be little doubt that he is already in the 'great' category. How could he not be after his performance in the second test against the Lions in 2005, an individual performance in a team game that would rank alongside Dave Loveridge's — also in a second test against the Lions — in 1983 and Jeff Wilson's one-man band for Otago against Wellington in 1997?

Carter himself would demur at any such talk. He would not like comparisons made between him and others and he does not like hearing or reading of himself in glowing terms. He is modest and understated; an unaffected young man who knows he has a job to do and does it at the best of his ability — which is considerable.

There's often talk about whether a player has the X factor, whatever that may be. It's called the X factor precisely because it defies rational and logical definition. It is something, whatever it may be, that sets one player apart from others. It's either there or it isn't and however hard it may be to describe it, it is remarkably easy to identify when it appears. There have been players over the years with the X factor. Players who, willingly or not, wilfully or not, stand out from the rest. Dan Carter is such a player.

Ron Palenski
July, 2006

Opposite page: Dan Carter in full stride against Wales at Cardiff's Millennium Stadium in 2005. The All Blacks won this match 41–3.

Skills

In this section of the book I try to explain various skills — I wouldn't be so presumptuous at my tender age to call this an instruction section or to say this is what a textbook says you must do. It is what I do.

The first thing, and this applies to any skill in any sport, is to practise, practise and practise again. The aim is to practise so often that when the skills are demanded under high pressure in a game, they come instinctively, almost without thinking. Ask yourself why the very best golfers, for example, head for the putting green or the practise tee almost as soon as they've finished a round. They know there's no substitute for practice, no replacement for repetitive hard work. If it were easy, we'd all be golf or tennis millionaires.

Under the enthusiastic tutelage of my father, I started learning the various rugby skills at a very young age and, since it was enjoyable, I just kept doing it. And doing it. As I became older, I realised what I needed to do to become a first-class rugby player and I practised even more; and once I became a professional player, I knew that practice was as much a part of my job as playing. It didn't matter how many goals I'd kicked or whatever, only constant practice and making a conscious action into an instinctive one was the only method that would succeed.

Another important point to remember is that there is no such thing as the perfect way to kick, just as there is no such thing as a perfect swing in golf. Certain principles apply

with every action but no one can ever reach the point at which they can say, 'There, I can do it now, I can stop practising'. The time to stop practising is the time to stop playing.

It's the principles of kicking or passing or tackling, or whatever, that a coach is referring to when he says his players 'can't even get the basics right'. It's the basics that are the cornerstone of success. And it's implanting the basics in your brain that leads to a player being able to use them instinctively in a game. If the fundamentals of an action are not mastered during practice, when conditions are usually as good as they'll ever get, they certainly won't be mastered in a game when conditions are determined by the opposition, the weather, the state of the game, the noise of the crowd — a whole range of uncontrollable factors. So at the risk of repeating myself: practise, practise, practise.

It's important too to warm up for kicking, whether for a match or just practice. You can do this with a friend or even up against a wall with short kicks of say five metres or so, kicking off both feet, exaggerating the action so you know that everything is in the working order that it is supposed to be.

Above: Taking a high ball during an All Black practice.
Left: Attacking a hit shield during Crusaders training.

KICKING

The drop punt

This has been in the game as long as I have been playing, but it wasn't so many years ago that the spiral was the only choice of kick for touch or for gaining territory. The advantage of the drop punt is that it is more accurate when executed properly and provides more consistency. Fewer variables affect it.

The ball is held perpendicular to the ground, that is, it points up and down. Hold the ball on either side and gently guide it with the right hand if a right-foot kicker. I'm a natural left-footer so I guide it with my left hand. Make sure the chest is front-on and that the shoulders are square-on to the target. Hold

the ball in front of the kicking leg and make sure the chest is over the planted foot. If the ball is not held over the kicking leg, it means your leg will have to come inward to connect with the ball and a sliced kick will probably result. The bottom of the ball should connect with the top of the foot just behind the toes and the follow-through is crucial. Follow the leg right through its arc and keep the toes of the kicking foot pointed toward the target.

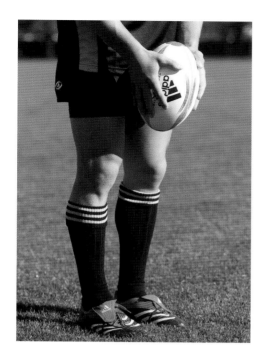

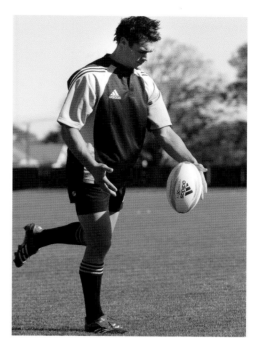

The spiral

This may not be the kick of first choice any more but properly struck, it still would win any prize for good looks. There's nothing better to watch than a perfectly struck spiral and if you're in the thin air of altitude at Johannesburg or Pretoria, so much the better. The advantage of the spiral over the drop punt is in aerodynamics — the ball spinning through the air gives it more distance and the same spinning action means it's faster through the air. It's used when you want to get the ball to some place in a hurry — to beat a fullback or wing running across in anticipation, for example. An advantage of the spiral is that it skids off the turf nicely and can add metres to your kick. There's also a kick called a spiral bomb that isn't often used in matches but when it is, it creates havoc among defenders because of its unpredictable flight and bounce.

The principles of the spiral are the same as for the drop punt, except for how the ball is held. For a left-foot kicker, the ball is held at an angle with the left hand at the back for guidance. Think of a clockface and think of five past seven. The right hand should be about where the one is, and the left hand at about where the seven is. Keep the body straight on and chest over the kicking foot. The top of your foot should connect with the sweet spot and you kick through the ball, following through with toes pointing at the target, exactly the same as with the drop punt.

Grubber kick

This is a tactical kick and the ball bounces end over end, making is easier to retrieve for the player following it up. Its disadvantage is that it is an easier kick for the opposition to charge down because of its low flight off the foot; so it's important when using it to take the ball right to the defending line and attack a hole, looking to kick it through. The kick is an ideal attacking weapon and is most commonly used within an opponent's 22.

The ball is held with hands either side, almost the same as with a drop punt but the foot connects more with a stab action, although it's still important to follow through (as well as remember the basics of body position). The key difference from the drop punt is that the ball is held at an angle of about 45 degrees and the foot connects with the top of the ball, rather than the bottom. The ball is usually struck closer to the ground as well. It's possible, with practice, to steer grubber kicks so the effect is rather like in-swingers and out-swingers in cricket. The nose of the ball should be pointed in the opposite direction to that in which you want the ball to go and you connect with the inside or outside of the foot, depending on whether you want it to go left or right.

The ball is usually struck closer to the ground.

It's still important to remember to follow through.

It's possible, with practice, to steer grubber kicks.

Dropkick at goal

Like the grubber, this is a kick in which the instincts must take over. If the basics and the timing haven't been honed in practice, the laughter of the crowd will ring in your ears. The difficulty with this kick is that the kicker receives the ball in such a variety of ways and seldom in the most ideal, controlled way. For every 10 dropkicks at goal, there are probably 10 different ways in which the

Tip

If you think you've mastered the dropkick, practise again. To practise dropkicking for goal, have someone pass the ball to you from different angles and heights.

ball will be received. A well-struck dropkick can win a match — there's no better example than Jonny Wilkinson in the World Cup final in 2003 — but it's a kick most commonly reserved for tight finishes. Teams naturally tend to try to score tries when they're on attack within their opponents' 22 and it's far better to go for a potential seven points than three. The chances of opponents infringing and giving away a potential three points for a penalty are usually greater than a dropkick at goal. In nearly 100 first-class matches, I've kicked four dropped goals, all of them for the Crusaders. Nevertheless, it does seem to have become an under-utilised way of scoring points.

The key to the dropkick is the drop of the ball. The ball should land on its point and the ideal is to strike the ball as it pops up. Try to drop the ball from lower down than for any other kick because it reduces the margin of error. The contact with the ball in a dropkick is the equivalent of a half-volley in tennis or cricket — connection with the ball is a split second after the bounce. It's important when receiving the ball for a planned dropped goal attempt that the body is already in as close to the correct position as possible — even the second or so it takes to change and prepare could be the second or so a defender needs to either tackle or get in a position to charge-down. And remember, the chances of a charge-down are greater because the kick is made from a lower angle.

Restarts

These also use the dropkick but are more controlled and controllable. With a restart, the kick is either for space, that is, long, or to regain possession on or just beyond the 10-metre line, which means the kick has to be higher. If you want the ball higher, kick under it more, give it more lift. Neither kick should be aimless, though — as with all kicks, fix the target in your mind and follow through with the toes pointing in the direction in which you want the ball to go.

Placekicks

These are the kicks which are seen to win matches, even though there are many other variables in a game that can determine the outcome. The placekicker in rugby is the most publicly exposed — and sometimes the most lonely — player on the field. All eyes and all cameras are on him when he places the ball, lines it up and kicks. Practice and instinct should be the constant companions of any placekicker. There are no hard and fast laws for placekickers once the principles are ingrained. Some players have particular foibles, some seem to have a different routine each time they kick and others copy what they see.

I have my own routine which I follow with every kick. The kicking tee is one for personal preference and I use what's known as the Super Tee. Most kickers start with a high tee, which is a great idea, but it's best to get to a low one as soon as confidence allows. In the end, though, what matters is what feels most comfortable for the individual. I place the ball pretty much straight up and down, but with a slight forward lean, with the valve facing the goalposts. The lean means the point of contact — the sweet spot — is opened up a little more. I take five paces back and then three to the right. This is when I visualise. I focus in on the left-hand upright, visualising where I want the ball to fly. I'm almost on my toes as I approach the ball at a controlled pace, my eyes are concentrated on the sweet spot at the bottom third of the ball.

Tip

Train as you would play. If practising kicking, practise as if it were in a game. If it helps, pretend the practise kick at goal you're about to make is winning the World Cup for the All Blacks.

I aim to connect with the inside of the foot, but back from the big toe. I lean slightly forward and my left shoulder should be over the ball. One arm goes out instinctively for balance. Ideally, my kicking foot — my left foot — is in contact with the ball for perhaps 12–15 centimetres, effectively guiding it. That makes the follow-through absolutely crucial. The timing is everything. It's not power that sends the ball on its way. It's the timing, the coming together of the left leg and the ball at precisely the right time. Try to kick the ball too hard and, more likely, power will be lost rather than gained because the body position will change.

I emphasise that's the way I do it, not how everyone should kick. All are different and all have different methods and within the established principles, there is no 'right' way or 'wrong' way. There are just successful kicks and unsuccessful kicks. Some teams have kickers who are used within, say, 40 or 45 metres of the posts, and then someone else is used for longer kicks, or even, on occasions, different kickers from different sides of the field. I back myself to kick a goal from anywhere within the half.

Tip

Practising goalkicking is the easiest because it is the same in practice as it is in a game: no defenders to worry about, just you, the ball and the posts. If you get it right in practice, you should get it right in a game.

Mick's the Man

Mick Byrne (right), the All Blacks' kicking coach, has an impressive pedigree in a sport that largely goes unnoticed in New Zealand.

He played 180 games in the AFL or, as it's more commonly known in New Zealand, Australian rules. He played for a New South Wales age grade side in an interstate carnival when he was 17 and so impressed scouts from the big clubs that he was signed by Melbourne. Over a long career through the 1970s and early 80s, he played for Melbourne and Hawthorne and then finished with the Sydney Swans. He won what every rules player covets, a premiership medal, when Hawthorne beat Essendon in the 1983 grand final.

Byrne played primarily as a ruckman, which is roughly equivalent to a rugby lock, at least in the physical requirements of the position, but also in the centre-half forward and full forward positions. The forward positions are those in which the basic requirement is to mark or otherwise receive the ball, and then kick the goals.

When he retired from playing, he turned to coaching specialist skills and before he joined the All Blacks as kicking coach, he'd had stints with teams in the AFL and league, and then with the Brumbies and the Wallabies. He joined the All Blacks from the Saracens club in England. He is the second specialist kicking coach with whom Dan Carter has been involved, the first being the former rugby and league player Daryl Halligan, during 2003. — *Ron Palenski*

allblacks

PASSING

Good, accurate passing is critical to the success of a team. It's simple really. The ball will beat the man every time — the ball can go through the air quicker than even the quickest of players can run and one of the fundamental aims of rugby is to create space and get to areas of the ground where the defenders are thinnest, and that leads to tries. Be careful of the weight — the speed — of the pass: too hard and a player may be caught unawares; too soft and it could put the receiver under pressure or, even worse, cause him to be intercepted. The more a player develops his passing, the better the chances of creating that extra space and time and the better the chances of scoring tries — and isn't that the goal of every team?

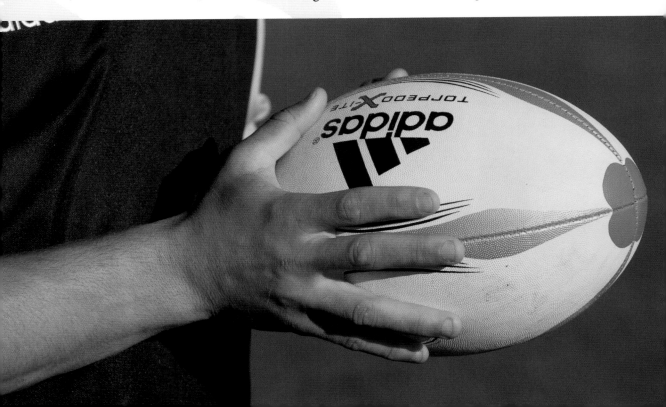

There are two basic types of pass: short and long. For the short pass, the hands should be on either side of the ball a little bit back from the middle and the thumbs spread. The ball should sit nicely in the palm, three or four centimetres from the heel of the hand. Follow through when the ball is released with the hands going toward the target. When receiving a pass, have the hands in the position ready to receive so the ball can be passed on that much quicker. Some experts say you've got to open up your hips to pass but the natural arc when passing is straight across, and your hips will naturally follow when following through. Some text books will say you've got to be careful where your feet are when passing but you'll find that the need for natural balance dictates where your feet go anyway and it's important when passing, as with most things, just to let the instinct take over rather than get bogged down trying to learn and recall a whole series of commands.

For the longer pass, one hand becomes the dominant hand. If you're passing to the right, all the control comes from the left hand and that's reversed if you're passing to the left. It shouldn't matter whether you're a natural left- or right-hander —

Tip

To help passing, build up wrist muscles by spinning a ball into the air as often as you can — even when watching TV. Just spin the ball one hand to the other — it will make a difference. Alternatives to a ball are the range of squeezing grips available at sports and fitness stores.

again, practice will make perfect. Passing to the right, the left hand does all the work and the right hand is there mainly for balance. The top hand — the worker hand — is at the base of the ball and you should use the fingers and wrist to impart spin on the ball to ensure both speed and accuracy. Again, it's important to follow through with both hands heading in the direction of the target. The head should ideally be balanced over the ball for greater accuracy, but as we all know, optimum conditions don't always apply in rugby.

TACKLING

There are two basic types of tackle, front-on and side-on, and then there are all manner of variations possible, both rehearsed and unrehearsed, legal and illegal. The essential aim is to stop the ball carrier and put him on the ground and while there is a variety of ways to do that, the most effective ways are the orthodox ways.

With the front-on tackle, I prefer to watch an opponent's hips and I get a fair idea of what they're going to do by that. It also tends to take my body lower into the tackle which, of course, is much preferred. A tackle from a standing position is much easier to brush off and, even if contact is made, it is unlikely a standing tackle will take a player to the ground. So I approach low, have a straight spine, chin up and watch the opponent's hips. I take short steps — allowing for quick adjustment — going into the tackle and get as close as I can with my leading foot before grabbing the opponent around the waist area. I keep my head to the side, wrap my arms around and then drive through with the legs to keep the power going.

> ## Tip
>
> In tackles, it's as important to get up as it is to get your opponent down. The player on his feet has all the rights, as referees like to say, so practise getting back to your feet with the intention of retrieving the ball as soon as you can.

With the side-on tackle, it's harder to get the timing right because of the differing speeds between the ball carrier and the tackler. It's necessary to adjust speed as you close in on the tackle to aid the timing. I get as close as I can then hit with the shoulder and wrap my arms around. I try to go cheek to hip, get a really good wrap, then slide my arms down. The positioning of the head in the tackle is of extreme importance. The last thing you want is your head jammed between the ground and the player you've tackled. Any attempted fend should be overcome by a good, low body position, short steps to allow a quick adjustment and the arms just wide enough apart to encircle the ball carrier. A tackler with arms wide apart can be fairly simply deflected.

Tip

Get hold of a rugby ball as often as you can. The more you handle a ball, the more adept you become with its use.

Black Dreams

I always wanted to be an All Black. Not that different from a lot of young boys in New Zealand, I don't suppose. For as long as I can remember, perhaps from when I was about five or six, it was an All Black I wanted to be when I grew up. Of course wanting was one thing; achieving was another. I just had this passion for rugby and, whenever I could, I'd have a rugby ball in my hands or at my feet.

I was born in Leeston, a nice little country town about 40 km south of Christchurch near Lake Ellesmere, in 1982, which, as I learned later, was a year in which the All Blacks regained the Bledisloe Cup from Australia. Perhaps that was a sign. There was nothing remarkable about my upbringing, nothing that set me apart from anyone else, and nothing I would change. My parents Neville, who is a builder, and Beverly, a teacher, provided a normal sort of New Zealand home and while I was growing up it all seemed pretty normal to me; it's only as I've travelled around a bit that I've come to realise how fortunate we in New Zealand are.

I have an older sister, Sarah, and I suspect Dad was pretty pleased when I came along because he was dead keen on his rugby and here was a son who could carry that passion on. Dad loved the game and loved being involved — he'd played for the Southbridge club and for Ellesmere and Canterbury Country. He was a proud Southbridge man and if I could also play at that level, then he'd be even more proud. I think he popped a rugby ball in my hands almost as soon as I was old enough to hold one.

Like most kids I suppose, especially those growing up in rural areas, my early life was a whirl of outdoor living involving any and every sport that was played, broken by the necessities of education. My mother saw to that. She was a relieving teacher at the time and occasionally she would arrive at Southbridge Primary School to fill in for absent teachers or for some other reason. When that happened, everyone knew Mrs Carter was Dan's mum and I'd sit in embarrassed silence as she patiently guided her young charges through another day of learning.

I dutifully did what was required of me at school but I lived for the times I could be outside. I just loved being involved in whatever was going and if it was rugby, so much the better. If perfection for a young boy is playing cricket in the summer and rugby in the winter, then I had perfection during my school days. I loved cricket as much as I did rugby. It was great just to be playing.

Though it was just something that happened then, I know now that it's important when you're growing up to try everything and, after a while, you'll know what you enjoy and of course if you're better at something, that always helps the enjoyment. I loved my cricket and continued to play through my school days as a middle-order batsman and a medium-pace bowler, but rugby was always No 1. The All Blacks were like some kind of gods, men of legend who I saw on television — I was five when New Zealand won the first World Cup — and when I played on my own, I'd kick and chase or fire out perfect passes, or step off both feet before scoring the winning try — all in the name of John Kirwan. The whistle — no sirens then — sounding the end of the game was Mum calling me in for tea, but there'd always be just time for one last run, one last kick.

As my body took shape, it became obvious that I would never be a lock or a prop, or even a forward of any description. But I always wanted to be a back anyway. My enthusiasm and love for the game always loomed larger than my bulk, or lack of it, and inevitably, I suppose, early teachers and coaches made me a halfback. Not that I minded. Halfbacks are always involved in the game and that's what I enjoyed. I don't know if there really is such a thing as natural talent or whether someone just gets immersed in sport because of the enjoyment factor and the longer they do it, and the more enthusiasm and dedication they show, the better they become. So I don't know if I was born with a rugby ball imprinted on my genes, but I do know I had enthusiasm and passion to burn and every time I had a chance to play, I'd play. This saw me playing for the Southbridge age grade team and then whatever representative age grade sides there were. I played for the Ellesmere under 10s when I was nine, so I played up a level and therefore against boys bigger than me, but it wasn't something that bothered me, or even something I can remember being conscious of. It was just another game of footy, other players with whom to play and others to beat, relishing the warm glow of victory and dreading that awful empty feeling that comes with losses.

It was when I was at Ellesmere College that a coach first suggested I play at first five-eighth, partly because, I suspect, he already had a halfback but he knew too that I had some ability as a goalkicker and there's a certain mindset in rugby that goalkickers should be

> **As my body took shape, it became obvious that I would never be a lock or a prop, or even a forward of any description.**

either fullbacks or first five-eighths. Not that I minded. I was just happy to play anywhere and in any case, a first-five is almost as much in the thick of the action as a halfback. My goalkicking was entirely self-taught. We had a piece of land next to our house and Dad cleared it and put up goalposts for me and when I wasn't stepping off both feet on my way to scoring winning tries, I'd spend countless hours kicking at goal. I tried setting the ball up the old way by digging a hole with my heel or by making a mound with the earth, but that didn't seem to work so well so I fashioned kicking tees out of anything I could find. This was in the late 1980s and early 1990s when kicking tees were the Big New Thing in rugby, introduced from Canada I think.

Ellesmere College was one of those secondary schools that began at form one, there being no intermediate schools in the area. I was chosen for the First XV when I was in the fourth form and while that may seem a young age to be footing it with the elite boys at the school, you've got to remember this was a country school and it didn't have the vast numbers from which to choose that a city school would.

I was still being chosen for wider age grade teams and the highlight of these was Country matches against Town. They were our grudge matches, the time when the Country boys would show the city slickers they were not a bunch of hicks. Well, sometimes. I think Town were usually too big and strong for us but every so often we'd pull off an upset and of course we'd feel like we'd just won the Ranfurly Shield and the Bledisloe Cup all on the same day. And there'd be mutterings from the Town guys. It was great.

Ellesmere College was a fairly new school and, outside of Canterbury, few people would probably have heard of it. It may not have ranked with the top rugby schools in New Zealand, but even so it can now claim two All Blacks. We didn't play the big boys such as Christchurch Boys' High School or St Andrew's or Christ's; they were way out of our league. Mt Hutt College in Methven was more our size. Although Ellesmere was firmly in Canterbury, and long may it remain so, for practical reasons we teamed up with Mid-Canterbury and, in 1999, I was chosen in a Hanan Shield districts team for a regional tournament that was played at St Bede's in Christchurch. I must have played quite well because from that side I made a Southern Region

Opposite page: Dad and Mum on the next-door ground where I used to practise.

School days. Ellesmere College and Temuka High School players greet each other after a game in 1997. I'm third from the left in the red and blue of Ellesmere.

schools team and we played in a tournament in Rotorua against Central and two Northern teams. It was then that I was also chosen as fullback for the first time. I'm not sure you could mention Don Clarke or Fergie McCormick or any other great fullback in the same breath as Daniel William Carter because then he was just a slightly-built youth who could play a bit.

After that, I was chatting with a friend from Ashburton High School who had also been in the Hanan Shield team and who was also madly enthusiastic about his rugby and we decided to spend our seventh form years at the holy of holies of Straven Road, Christchurch Boys' High School. It would be good for our rugby because we'd be in a higher level of competition and, of course, there'd be much greater competitiveness for a place in teams. Parents were consulted, schools were consulted and the change took place, and I'll always be grateful to the people at Ellesmere College for being so helpful and supportive.

It was a daunting move. From the country to the city. From Ellesmere College, proud

Sport helped in the big transition from country to city. I'm second from right in the back row, in the Christchurch Boys' High School first XV, 2000.

but unnoticed by the general populace, to one of the great schools of New Zealand, a school proud of its history and traditions and anxious that every one of its pupils carry the torch on for the next generation. I may have looked confident and poised on the rugby or cricket fields, but I was anything but when I walked through the gates of CBHS for the first time. It was scary. Quite apart from the demands of such a school, it was so crowded compared with what I had been used to.

I always bore Dad's advice in mind — and still do! Just get on with what you have to do, do what you're told and just keep quiet until you have something to say that's worth saying. It was good advice.

So I was petrified when I first went to school in the city, but forever grateful and pleased that I did. Sport always helps in such a big transition. It was still the cricket season of course at the start of the year and I was chosen for the First XI, and that helped establish

me at the school, even if I was there only a year. As much as I loved cricket, summer to me then was but the waiting time before winter and rugby. The school's reputation in rugby was immense and I remember standing one day by an honours board that listed all of the school's All Blacks. The list seemed to go on forever and, like most teenagers, I was steeped in the playing of rugby rather than its history.

Though still small — some might say weedy — I entered the rugby season with enthusiasm and I was determined that I wouldn't let myself down or my parents and others who had supported and encouraged me. I played the series of trials and made the First XV and so finally was able to play against the 'big' schools which were beyond the reach of Ellesmere College. I also made the Canterbury Secondary Schools team and Southern Regions.

The national secondary schools team that year went to Australia but I was barely conscious of it. I don't think I was ever in contention for it and I certainly never had any expectations of being selected. That and New Zealand Under 19, which played in the world championship in France, were a level beyond me. The only players from the CBHS First XV that year who did make the national secondary schools side were my good friend from Ashburton, Ben Jones, and Adam Thomson, a flanker who later moved to Otago.

I finished school at the end of the year and started working as a labourer for Dad, not at all sure if I would be good enough to be a professional footballer and not knowing what I would end up doing as a real job. By this time, I was flatting in Christchurch and in 2001 I played for the High School Old Boys club. I played for their Colts team mostly though I had a few games at Senior B and Senior level and was chosen for Canterbury Under 19. I was selected for the Canterbury Academy and this, probably more than anything, shaped my rugby future. It was still not professional rugby, not even fulltime rugby, but it was rugby of an intensity that I had not had before. It was a huge step for me. Under the guidance of Rob Penney, I was training now for rugby in the summer months, something I had never done before. I was introduced to gymnasiums, which previously had been foreign territory to me.

Opposite page: Annual clash — on attack for Christchurch Boys' High School against Christ's College in 2000. Christ's won 19–8 on this occasion.

Into Red and Black

The Super 12 still had a Development competition in 2002. It was the equivalent of the NPC Development competition or of provincial B teams. I think there were various rules at times restricting the Super 12 Development by age, but with some exceptions. The Development teams played curtain-raisers to the Super 12 games but, without Australian and South African involvement, it was obviously a shorter competition. It was, in any case, a step immediately below first-class rugby and important for any player aspiring to a professional career in rugby.

Being in the Canterbury Academy meant you were noticed by important people in rugby and they thought you had something of a future and the idea of the Academy was to prepare the young players for later rugby life. When coaches needed players for whatever team, they would run their eyes over the Academy players and ask penetrating questions about how this player was shaping up or how that player was coping. Being a young and quiet player, I didn't know any of these things but someone must have been asking questions about me because I played in trials for the Crusaders Development team and then, when injury created an opening, I was given a chance by coaches Greg Coffey and Ian Mallard. Two first five-eighths, Cameron McIntyre and Charles Hore, had been chosen for the Development team but both were injured and I was called in. It was a great thrill because it was the best team I'd made up to that stage of my career, but it was also very sobering; this was make or break time. If I could play reasonably well and not make any, or at least many, outlandish mistakes, I might be called on again. If I proved to be incapable of handling rugby at this higher level, in

Although I was a late call-up for the Development team, I ended up playing all four games. We lost only once . . .

all probability I would not receive a second invitation. This is what sport is like. When chances are given, they have to be taken. An opportunity that is missed may not arise again.

While I was thrilled to be given such a chance, so were my flatmates. Being students, they were usually broke so they were delighted that I was for the first time being paid as a rugby player — Development players received a small allowance — but I think even more delighted when I arrived back at the flat one day with all the gear with which I'd been issued. Polo shirts and rain jackets with new labels still hanging off them are not something students see very often, if at all, and of course, being a student flat, clothes were something to be shared around. I did as much sharing as I was able without compromising the 'dress of the day' requirements of the team.

Although I was a late call-up for the Development team, I ended up playing all four games. We lost only once, to the Chiefs at Jade, and finished up winning the competition,

Playing for the Crusaders Development team in their opening game of the 2002 competition against the Highlanders. The Crusaders won 28–26.

just edging out the Highlanders. It was quite a tight final day. The Highlanders beat the Chiefs in Invercargill in the afternoon and earned a bonus point and that meant we, in Auckland that night, had to have a bonus point win over the Blues to secure the title. This we were able to do, winning 41–5 after leading 14–5 at halftime. I thoroughly enjoyed the experience of playing in such a competition and was satisfied with the manner in which I had played and, of course, it always helps if the goalkicking works. I ended up as the leading points scorer in the competition with 43.

Although it was supposed to be a 'B' competition, some pretty talented players were involved, certainly quite the best company in which I had played. The Crusaders, for example, included players such as Orene Ai'i, Jamie Nutbrown, Campbell Johnstone, Chris King and Johnny Leo'o. The Blues, who we beat in the last round, were captained by Daniel

Braid and included Anthony Tuitavake, Sam Tuitupou, Justin Collins, Sione Lauaki and Angus Macdonald, so clearly there were some very talented players involved.

Being involved at that level and playing reasonably well came as a bit of a shock to me. Obviously I'd aspired to play at the highest level I could, but achieving that goal is something I never took for granted. Rugby's more than just about lacing up boots. It was probably my experience in those early months of 2002 that made me realise for the first time that I could really become a fairly decent footballer and perhaps play the game professionally. It gave me a taste and I wanted more.

It wasn't back to High School Old Boys either. Soon after the Super 12, I was invited — I like the way rugby uses the word 'invited'; as if anyone would ever turn down such an invitation — to trials in Palmerston North for the national under-21 team to go to the international tournament in South Africa. I didn't have any great expectations because I still had a year up my sleeve to play for the Colts and I just assumed there were older and better players than me in contention, including a few who had played in the Super 12. But just the chance to play in trials at a national level was another step in the right direction. I played in the trial and it was a bit of a surprise — more than a bit — when the team was named after the trial and my name was read out. I had been chosen for my first national team!

There wasn't any chance to dwell on it, or to celebrate with parents and family and friends, because the chosen 29 — 13 backs and 16 forwards — went direct from Palmerston North to Auckland and then on to South Africa. It was the first time I'd been on a rugby trip outside of New Zealand. The other players and the team management, led by a legend of the game, Sean Fitzpatrick, were welcoming but I felt unsure about my place in the setup. I kept imagining that other players looked at me sideways and muttered to themselves, 'How did he get in the team? What's he done?' If anyone had been asked to name the leading under-21 players in the country at the time, I'm quite sure no one would have come up with my name. No one had heard of me. But I supposed that the coach, Bryce Woodward, and his assistant, Dennis Brown, had come up with my name and, as unsure as I may have been, it was up to me to show that I was worthy of a place.

I guess I was chosen as a bit of a spare parts player and for goalkicking because there were two other first five-eighths ahead of me, Cameron McIntyre from Canterbury and

The 2002 NEW ZEALAND UNDER-21 TEAM

Back row: Sione Lauaki, Brad Mika, Ross Kennedy, Angus Macdonald, Joe Rokocoko. **Third row:** Mark Plummer (physio), Tom Harding, Jimmy Cowan, Tony Woodcock, Alfred Pelenise, Chris King, Daniel Braid, Thomas Waldrom, Bruce Hodder (video analyst). **Second row:** Brendan Ratcliffe (trainer), Ben Atiga, Shaun Webb, Peter Chaplin, Daniel Carter, Tim Fairbrother, Luke McAlister, Cameron McIntyre, Jamie Nutbrown, Peter Coleman (doctor). **Front row:** Sean Fitzpatrick (manager), Sam Tuitupou, Anthony Tuitavake, Warren Smith, Bryce Woodward (coach), Jason Shoemark, Simon Lemalu, Rhyan Caine, Dennis Brown (assistant coach). **Absent:** Corey Flynn, Casey Laulala, Lifeimi Mafi, Kane Thompson.

Luke McAlister from North Harbour. As it turned out, each of them was hampered by injury — McIntyre played in only the first game and McAlister the second, third and fourth, but the latter two as a substitute. Whether by accident or design, I became the team's first five-eighth and started in four of the games and went on in the fifth.

I thought we were the team of the tournament. We beat England 67–23 in the first game, Japan 99–8 in the second and Wales 73–19 in the third, which put us in a semi-final against South Africa. We should have beaten them and made the final, but we didn't. We led until late in the game but then François Swart kicked two penalty goals for them and it was a huge disappointment for us. It's not much consolation, as the All Blacks well knew, being the best team in a world competition if you don't actually win it. As Fitzpatrick told

us — and who would know better than him? — competing at the World Cup was all about making and winning the final. 'We came to South Africa to play in the final and win,' he said. 'It didn't happen. Those in this team will learn the lessons.'

I was happy enough with my own form, and even happier with the experience I gained. I was the top points scorer for the tournament with 68 but that's not much consolation when you lose. Personal milestones and achievements may be nice, but they count for nothing when your team loses.

So it was a trip that was a mixture of disappointment at the outcome but satisfaction at the experience gained. It was also a trip on which, I suppose, I became better known as a rugby player but one too that also produced some lasting friendships. That's one of the great things about rugby. The friendships you make, whether with your own team-mates or the opposition, last the rest of your days. It was something that was brought home to me in South Africa. One of my great friends is Joe Rokocoko and it was on that trip that I first met him. We've been close ever since and I've visited Fiji with him, meeting his relatives and friends and learning a little about the Fijian way of life and culture. I wouldn't have been able to do that but for the opportunities provided by rugby.

I think too the experience of that trip to South Africa showed me what a close-knit family rugby in New Zealand really is. We may be on opposite sides from time to time, but we're all New Zealanders with shared interests and passions. I've played with and against many of my under-21 team-mates since . . . Ben Atiga, Jimmy Cowan, Luke McAlister, Cameron McIntyre, Alfred Pelenise, Joe Rokocoko, Jason Shoemark, Anthony Tuitavake, Sam Tuitupou, Shaun Webb, Daniel Braid, Tim Fairbrother, Corey Flynn, Ross Kennedy, Chris King, Sione Lauaki, Angus Macdonald, Brad Mika, Tony Woodcock. It's a brotherhood of rugby.

The dream of fulltime rugby came even closer when I got home from South Africa and the Canterbury coach, Aussie McLean, included me in a wider training group for the NPC. The wider group was necessary because of the large number of Canterbury players away with the All Blacks and I thought that I would probably get a game or two until they

Opposite page: Getting the ball wide in the New Zealand Colts' 73–19 win against Wales in South Africa in 2002. Halfback Jimmy Cowan follows up.

returned and then I would be out, or playing for Canterbury B. Not that that would have worried me. I would still have been playing.

The inclusion in the wider group gave me my first rugby contract. Signing on the dotted line for Canterbury was a real thrill and something I thought might never happen. The amount of money wasn't huge but that was irrelevant. I know people today think that All Blacks make heaps of money but I also know that I, and others, would play for nothing just for the honour and satisfaction of playing for the All Blacks. In that respect, we're no different from the hundreds of All Blacks who came before and did play for nothing, and often at considerable cost to themselves.

July 17, 2002, is a date that will stick in my memory. That was the date on which I made my first-class debut for Canterbury, running onto Lansdowne Park in Blenheim as a substitute. Not just a first-class debut, but also a Ranfurly Shield debut. Canterbury had won the shield from Waikato in 2000, defended it through the 2001 season, and was now beginning its 2002 defences with an away game in Blenheim. Could it get any better than this? Well, yes it could. We were well in control of the game when I went on and slotted into second five-eighth, a position in which McLean said he would like me to have more experience.

We actually led 38–0 when I took the field and had been held at that score for some time by a very determined Marlborough defence, no doubt set their tasks emphatically by their coach, Alex Wyllie, who was well used to Canterbury ways. Quite by chance, I broke what had become something of a deadlock. The first time I received the ball I sensed a chance, stepped inside and scored. First game for Canterbury, first shield match, first touch, first try. Such fulfilment of dreams surely couldn't last. It was like living out in reality those imagined games of long before on the field next door to home in Southbridge.

I had two more shield matches and started both at second five-eighth, the first against Mid-Canterbury in Ashburton and the second my Canterbury debut at Jade against East Coast. They went well for me because I scored twice in Ashburton and then three times at Jade but, more importantly, the team was also performing well. I retained my place for the first of the NPC games, away against Wellington, but I expected that would be my last for a while because the All Blacks, or at least some of them, were returning the next week. We lost to Wellington so we were a fairly pensive group when we met on the Sunday morning to hear McLean tell us who was in the squad for the balance of the NPC.

Was someone injured I didn't know about? Was I there just for a short time filling a gap?

You know the old expression about a jaw dropping when something surprising is said? Well, if jaws really do drop, mine did. McLean read out the list of names and there among them was 'Dan Carter'. Was someone injured I didn't know about? Was I there just for a short time filling a gap? But no, McLean had me there as either a first five-eighth or second five-eighth, plus a backup goalkicker to Ben Blair, who had been doing a great job while the All Blacks were away, and to Andrew Mehrtens, who would do a great job whenever asked.

Not for the first time, and not for the last, I felt like an intruder, a third former who had somehow wandered into the prefects' room and was looking for the easiest way out without

Opposite page: Shield try — heading for my first try for Canterbury in the Ranfurly Shield defence against Marlborough at Blenheim in 2002.

being noticed. At the first training of the new squad, a glance around the dressing room was daunting: there was Justin Marshall, and there was Andrew Mehrtens, who I at least knew through the High School Old Boys club. And there was Norm Maxwell. Scott Robertson, more than 50 games for Canterbury. Mark Hammett. And others. What on earth, I wondered, was I doing here among such men? These were heroes, these were television men, men with whom unknown 20-year-olds didn't dare associate. This was the top table and here I was. I didn't dare utter a word. I was quite happy just to sit quietly in a corner, think about my own game and what was required of me, and speak when I was spoken to.

The Canterbury players, though, are a great bunch of blokes. They soon made me feel welcome by not treating me as anything special; just another team-mate, one they would look after when necessary and one, when the circumstances warranted, who they relied on to look after them. All for one and one for all. The essence of a team. I was apprehensive, but I was comfortable. This was what I had worked toward.

Even given my relative youth and inexperience, I'd realised that the level of rugby determines what is required from an individual. In school games and in some others, other players looked to me for guidance, to make the calls or to pull off some play that might make the difference between winning and losing. At this level, I could just concentrate on my own game; no one would be looking toward the youngest member of the team to guide them through troubled times. All that was required of me was to do my job. Aussie McLean, a shrewd coach and judge of footballers, knew how I would be feeling and he was prepared to allow me to find my feet in my own time. He was neither too demanding nor too lax in his demands of me. He'd seen what he thought were some qualities in my game and knew that, given time, those qualities would surface or, if they didn't, that would be proof enough that I wasn't up to it. I knew that myself. Everything in front of me was up to me.

McLean tried the sink or swim approach for the second NPC match, against Bay of Plenty in Rotorua. I was picked at first five-eighth with that wily old campaigner, Daryl Gibson, outside me. So much for easing me into it. I was on the bench for the next two games when the old firm of Marshall and Mehrtens was back in harness, but for the following game, against Northland, I was again at first five-eighth, playing outside Marshall

My first start at first five-eighth for Canterbury in the NPC match against the Bay of Plenty in 2002. Canterbury won 35–30.

for the first time. Veteran halfbacks can be hard on rookie first-fives who don't stand in the right places, don't run the right lines, but Marshall gave me a dream run and helped considerably to ease the qualms I still felt at playing in such company. As the NPC neared its climax, I was the boy apprentice studying at the feet of masters. Sometimes in the team, sometimes on the bench, always in the dressing room, always learning. We gained a home semi-final that year but lost to Auckland. I went on as a substitute so gained another new experience, that of finals rugby, in a year full of new experiences.

Not long after the NPC, and before Robbie Deans went off to Europe with the All Blacks, he phoned me and asked if I could go to his office. I barely knew him at that stage. I think we'd been introduced but that was about it. He was way above my station in life. So off I went, as apprehensive as if I'd been summoned by the headmaster. He told me he was going to pick me in the Crusaders for the Super 12 in 2003. He said some nice things about the way I'd played in the NPC and advised me to listen to what was happening around me, to learn as much about rugby as I could, to train hard and push the players ahead of me. He told me I might find it a bit daunting, but he was confident I would make it. A bit daunting! Once again, I was left wondering what on earth I'd be doing in such company. But here I was. Just a year after playing Colts rugby for High School Old Boys, I was now a professional rugby player. I was now a Crusader. I was now a Super 12 player, contracted to that mystical body in Wellington about which I knew little, if anything — the New Zealand Rugby Union. There was just one word I could find to describe how I felt. Awesome.

The Crusaders started training in December of 2002 and I did every session possible from then until the competition started in February. I worked hard in the gym and I worked hard at training. And when team training was finished, I stayed out on the field practising goalkicking or line kicking or up-and-under. Or anything. I worked and I worked. No one told me to do that. I just did it because I enjoyed it and because

There are no half measures in a game; there can't be any half measures in training.

it was part of my job, my game. It was tiring though. I was knackered. Sometimes between sessions I'd go back to the flat and have a sleep, just to recover in time for the next one. There are no half measures in a game; there can't be any half measures in training. That's what I told myself as I pushed myself again and again.

We had some warmup games in Australia and I felt I played reasonably well although you're never sure after such games because different combinations are tried, subs are coming and going and it never feels like a real game. But I thought, as we prepared for the opening match against the Hurricanes, that I was as ready as I could be to sit on the bench and watch and learn and do whatever was required of me. The team to play the opening match was named and I was in it at first five-eighth. I'd had no warning; the team had no warning — the whole of New Zealand had no warning. 'Who's this kid who's taken the spot

My Super 12 debut for the Crusaders, against the Hurricanes in 2003. Here I get past wing Neil Brew. Luke Andrews, Christian Cullen and Tana Umaga pursue.

that Andrew Mehrtens had almost by right?' they must have asked. I must admit I asked myself the same question. Mehrtens was Mehrtens. A nice, decent man. He must have been hurting inside, but he was the first to congratulate me and throughout the season he was always there to help me, to give me encouragement and the odd hint. Mehrtens that year, more than any other, showed what a great bloke he is.

I don't think I've ever been as nervous as I was before that first game for the Crusaders against the Hurricanes. At least it was at Jade, where I could bank on a friendlier reception than I would ever find at the Westpac Stadium in Wellington. I'm not the type who wants to vomit before matches but there are times when I go to the toilet frequently before a game, and this was one of those times. I listened attentively to all the talk in the hotel

and in the dressing room before the game, and while we were waiting to go out, I swung my leg through in simulated goal kicks. To no avail as it turned out because I missed a couple of kicks early on, I think through sheer nervousness. But once the game's flow got going, I seemed to settle down. Aaron Mauger was injured and replaced by Mehrtens so I moved to second-five and I think that helped me as well. Mehrtens did the goalkicking so I just had to concentrate on playing my game. It helped that we gradually got on top of them and had a reasonably good win and I was lucky enough to score two tries and, more importantly, not do anything dumb that would have let the team down. There could have been nothing worse.

I ended up playing every game in my first year, six more at second-five and the others at first five-eighth, becoming the more or less regular goalkicker as well although Mehrtens still kicked in some games and Leon MacDonald did as well. I lost my nervousness and gained in confidence as the competition wore on. I was comfortable with the way in which I was playing and, more significantly, comfortable with the players I had around me. It was a great team to be part of. We beat the Hurricanes again in a semi-final at Jade but lost the final at Eden Park to the Blues. It wasn't a good way to end the season but overall it had been a satisfactory campaign. The amount of game time I had, as surprising as it was to me, helped me a lot and I was a more assured footballer by the end. I think it helped me too that, because it was my first year, I wasn't known all that well by the opposition players and I wasn't targeted as much as I would be in later years. Why should opponents then have targeted me anyway when they had backs such as Justin Marshall and Andrew Mehrtens to concentrate on? I was the new boy feeling his way; the opposition had bigger fish to fry.

If ever I'd had any doubts about my desire to be a professional rugby player, and if ever I'd wondered whether I could make it, I think that first season erased them. My desire was never seriously in question and, without wishing to sound big-headed about it, I think I showed that I was competent enough to play Super 12. I was exhausted, but happy. Having tasted it once, I wanted more the next year.

Opposite page: Happiness is . . . Congratulated by Caleb Ralph and Aaron Mauger after scoring my first try for the Crusaders. This was my first Super 12 game, against the Hurricanes.

A Dream Comes True

When the All Blacks coach, John Mitchell, was naming his first squad for the year in 2003, my mind was on bizarre clothing. It certainly wasn't on the All Blacks. It's the tradition with the Crusaders — and all teams have similar traditions — at the end of the Super 12, win or lose, to have a break-up day. It's a day when players relax and have a good time, knowing they don't have training the next day or a game the following weekend. The call for the Crusaders' break-up in 2003 was to wear something outlandish. I went off to lunch with a couple of mates as I pondered what to beg or borrow to make me look suitably ridiculous, but sufficiently muted as well so I could slip into the background if I felt the need.

Some people had mentioned to me that I might be a contender for the All Blacks, but I didn't believe that for a minute. The All Blacks? Me? One day perhaps, but not yet. Not after just one season of NPC and one of Super 12. There were lots of good players in my positions, either first or second five-eighth, whom Mitchell would pick ahead of me, surely. I barely gave the All Blacks team announcement a thought as I wondered about my wardrobe.

I was sitting having lunch when my cellphone went. It was Dad. 'Congratulations!' he shouted. 'You're in the All Blacks!'

I've been asked many times what I thought, how I felt, when I first heard the news that every New Zealand rugby player dreams of, fantasises about. I think I was stunned at first, understanding yet not quite comprehending what my father was saying. I must admit it flashed through my mind that there might have been some mistake but no, Dad wouldn't have got it wrong.

It came down to satisfaction, I suppose, which is such a bland word to describe an emotion that is just about indescribable. Pride? Yes, there was pride there. Elation? Of course. But I

think amid all those emotions there was too a growing awareness of what it meant — the sense of responsibility, the fact I was being entrusted to do something that rugby players anywhere would love to do. I could not let myself down, I could not let my parents and family down, or my friends, but most of all I could not let the All Blacks down. Rugby is the ultimate of team games and the All Blacks are the ultimate of teams. Their stature has been founded on the sweat and hard work of many men and, in a sense, I was required to carry on that work. So I think, amid all the excitement, there was a deep sense of commitment.

These were the types of thoughts which raced through my mind as I answered call after call — I don't think the cellphone had ever been so overworked — and as I made my way to Jade for one of the first jobs as an All Black, fronting up to the news media. I hadn't had much to do with reporters before, just the odd comment after a match, and of course I was still only 21 so hardly experienced in firing off sound grabs and quotable quotes. Brad Thorn was another new All Black from the Crusaders so his presence took a little of the heat off me. I was the new boy but he was the bigger story because he had previously turned down a chance to be an All Black because he wasn't sure he was committed to rugby or whether he would return to league. It had been a big call for Brad to make but the fact he made it indicated what sort of person he is.

We joined our Crusaders team-mates and there were a few celebratory drinks — and a few laughs at what some of the guys wore — but as far as I was concerned, and I suspect this applied to a few others too, the celebrating was measured because we had some hard physical and mental work coming up. For a rugby player, the job is never quite finished.

You remember how I said I felt when I first joined the New Zealand Under 21s, when I first joined the Canterbury NPC team, when I first joined the Crusaders? The feeling was even more intense when I joined the All Blacks. There was trepidation and nervousness, all the while wondering about my place in such company. I can't remember my first day at school as a five-year-old, but I'm sure it would have been something like how I felt when I checked in as an All Black. This time, though, there was no Mum waving from the gate, no chance to burst into tears and bolt into some comforting arms.

Opposite page: All Blacks coach John Mitchell and captain Reuben Thorne at the Wellington press conference when I was selected for the first All Blacks squad of 2003.

There was comfort though. Joe Rokocoko, my mate from the under 21s, was a new boy too, as was Ma'a Nonu, and the three of us gravitated toward each other, finding safety in numbers. Such feelings for new players are probably inevitable, but the older players couldn't have been more welcoming. It helped, of course, that quite a few of them were Crusaders whom I knew well but the experienced guys from other areas were just as supportive and welcoming. Whatever our backgrounds and our differences, all were set aside now for the greater good of the All Blacks. That was all that mattered.

Youthful and green I might have been, but I knew that being selected for the All Blacks was only a step along the way. Once you're in a wider squad, you've got to strive to get chosen for the playing team and the way you do that is to do what's asked of you and to challenge yourself continually in training. And when you're selected for the team, you've got to play well. And when you've played, and when you've really qualified for the title of 'All Black', you then strive to stay there and to be a better All Black. There's no room in such a team for players who think selection is the ultimate. Selection is just the opportunity.

The first task for the year was against England in Wellington, which was rather an unusual start. The normal pattern is to play less challenging teams and for the coaches to try and give everyone in the squad a game. And while the All Blacks always take every opponent with the utmost seriousness, there are some who clearly are a more daunting challenge than others. England was one of those. They fancied themselves and, since this was World Cup year, they were after a psychological leg-up against us.

As one of the new boys, I didn't think I would be involved against England and that my main mission at the time was to soak up the atmosphere of being in the All Blacks' camp and to learn. I was a little surprised, therefore, that I was named on the bench, which can bring with it its own pressure. You're not in the starting XV but you have to be prepared to go on, even in the first seconds of a game if needed. As it turned out, Carl Hoeft, Brad Thorn and I were the only three reserves who didn't get on, so we spent the whole time watching from the touchline as the game slipped away. The All Blacks lost 15–13.

My new team-mates were gutted. I was too, but perhaps not as much as them because I hadn't been a part of the game. The All Blacks dressing room is not a fun place to be after a loss. No one likes losing, the All Blacks least of all. The All Blacks don't lose all that often but when they do, it hurts. You sit there in the dressing room, usually head in hands, not daring to say anything for fear of breaking the heavy silence. Any conversations are brief and quiet. As a player, you wonder what you could have done better, how you could have perhaps prevented the loss. If you made a mistake, you think about it, analyse it, not in self-recrimination but in order to eliminate the possibility from the next game. The depression after a loss takes a while to lift.

I could not afford to dwell on the loss. I'd been told that I would be in the team the following week against Wales in Hamilton and sure enough, when the team was named on the Sunday, I was. There was time now only to think about what I had to do. I'd been named at second five-eighth outside Carlos Spencer and inside Tana Umaga and told that I would probably be doing the goalkicking as well. So began a week of training, thinking, nervous energy, and a week that led to the fulfilment of a dream. How it would turn out was entirely up to me, no one else.

> **As a player, you wonder what you could have done better, how you could have perhaps prevented the loss.**

The fact the opponents were Wales was irrelevant. Did I think about how they'd run the All Blacks close just a few months before in Cardiff only to see the score balloon out toward the end? No, I didn't give that a thought. That was then, this was now.

Did I spend time thinking of the great history of Wales, of players such as Gareth Edwards, Barry John, Phil Bennett, J.P.R. and the rest? Did I think about how for all the Welsh greatness and the intensity of the rivalry between our two countries, they hadn't beaten the All Blacks for 50 years? No, not a thought. Did I look at Robbie Deans and think that his great-uncle all those years ago in 1905 had had a try snatched away from him, thereby denying the first All Blacks an unbeaten tour? Did I think about the Welsh emotion, the singing, the giant leeks, the lilting accents? No, I didn't think about any of those things.

My thoughts in that week leading up to the test in Hamilton were entirely selfish. I concentrated, as players must, on my own game. I did everything I could to ensure that

Test debut.

Top: Lining up a kick for goal.

Above: Caught this time.

Right: Scoring my first test try, against Wales at Hamilton in 2003. Welsh fullback is Rhys Williams.

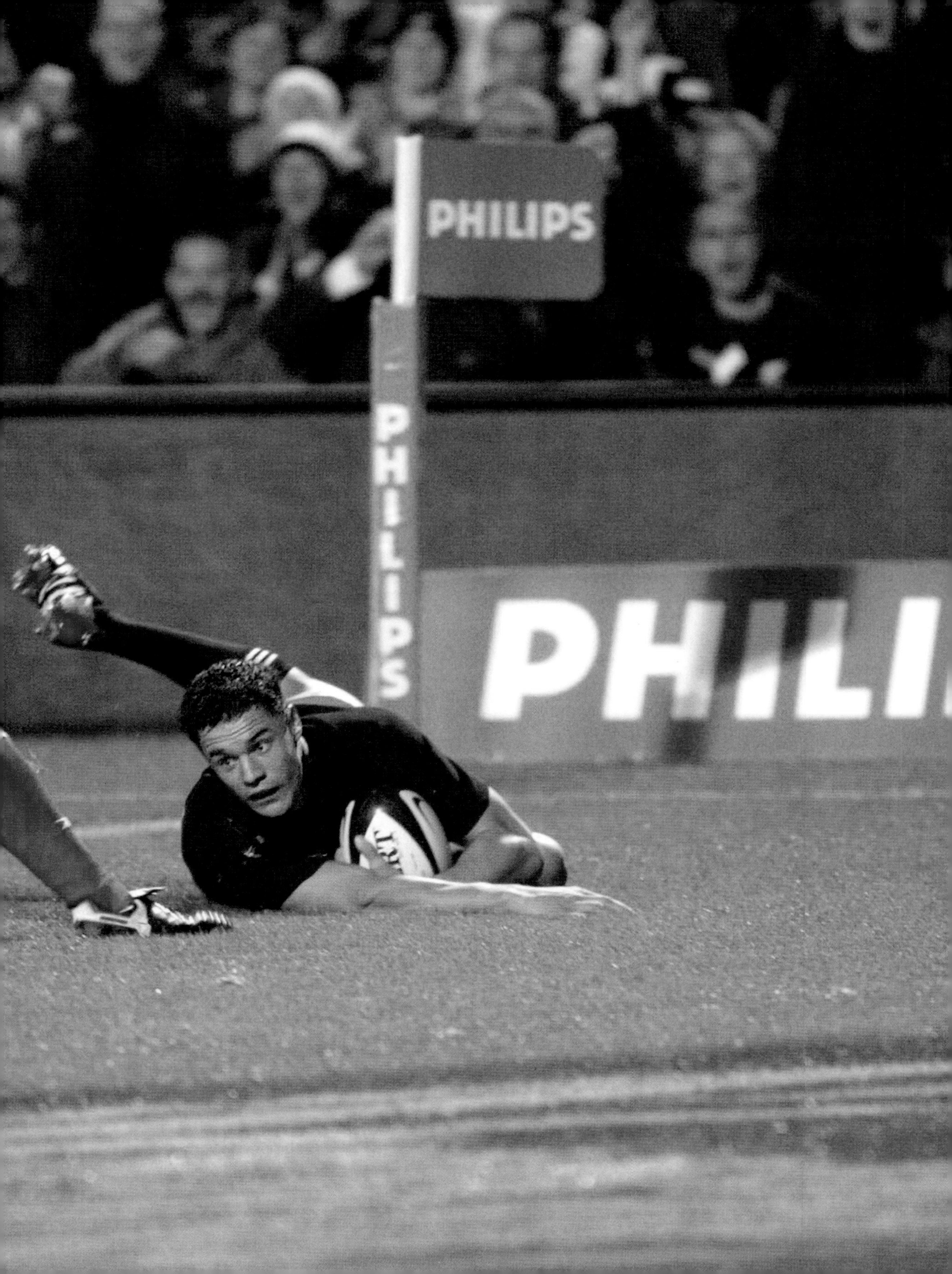
PHILIPS
PHILIPS

I was as ready as I would ever be. Nothing must be left to chance. I trained with the team, I trained on my own, I practised kicking under the expert eye of Daryl Halligan, the All Blacks' kicking coach. I talked to the other players about the moves and the calls, about what we would do if this happened, about how we'd respond if that happened. My thoughts were totally absorbed by the prospect of my first 80 minutes of test rugby.

About the only intrusion into this total rugby focus was the need to practise the haka and though that's not part of the game, it's an integral part of being an All Black.

The day of a night test can sometimes seem drawn out. You're all keyed up ready to play but you've got to fill in the day. There are team meetings, meals, checking gear, a few passes and walking through moves, lying on the bed watching television, the eyes seeing but the mind not following. It's become something of a recent trend in rugby for players from the past or notable figures from other walks of life to hand out the test jerseys. In Hamilton, we were presented with our jerseys by the squash player, Leilani Joyce. She knew the seriousness of the moment; she knew how significant it was, especially for the new boys such as me. She handed me my jersey — My Jersey! — neatly folded and with the No 12 uppermost. She wished me luck and I think I just mumbled a thanks. There was a tumbling of emotions, the reverence of handling the jersey mixed with the need still to think only of the game.

The day of a night test can sometimes seem drawn out. You're all keyed up ready to play but you've got to fill in the day.

Back to the room, then a team meeting, then the bus to the ground. Absolute silence on the bus. A few well-wishers standing outside the stadium as we pulled out, their cries of good luck shouted above the whoosh of the air brakes. File into the dressing room, still silence. Dump our bags in our designated places and file out again to look at the ground, to stand around. As a kicker, I tested the wind, moved about the ground, analysing its direction. Then back into the dressing room and change into All Blacks gear. Back out onto the ground for warm-ups which releases some of the pent-up mental energy. Running, passing, the ball in hand, a few kicks — all help ease the nerves, though not that much. I was nervous, no doubt about it. I just wanted the game to be over.

The final preparations, the last words, and the manager, Tony Thorpe, says from the door, 'Two minutes'. Reuben Thorne calls us into a huddle, says a few words but we each have our own thoughts. Then he heads for the door, takes a match ball from Thorpe's hands and out we go, into the night of expectation, of hopes, of exposure. Even though we've been out there for warm-ups, there's still a different feeling when you're out there for the real thing. Some players do some last-minute stretching, some snatch up some blades of grass, there's a few rapid passes, then line up for the national anthems. 'Land of My Fathers', as stirring an anthem as it may be, went by with me barely noticing. Thoughts on the game. Then 'God Defend New Zealand', singing the words I'd learnt so long ago at school. Then the haka, my first. I found some room toward the back but I really got into it and it pumped me up for what was to follow.

At last. Older hands had told me that test matches go by in a blur; they're played at a much faster pace than anything else. I think on the whole that's true. There's certainly an intensity unlike any other game and generally they are faster, more urgent. There are no second chances, no competition points or a chance to make up next week. It's here and now.

Being back in the dressing room after a win is much different from being there after a loss, that's for sure. There's a lot more talk, and most of it animated; there's back-slapping and a general feeling of a job well done. Individual players when they're unwinding their strapping — that's usually the forwards — or getting changed reflect on their own games, thinking about what they'd done and what they could have done better. I was content. Everything had flowed pretty well and the life of the backs was made much easier by our forwards having a good control of the game, especially after the testing-each-other-out period of the first 20 minutes or so.

I didn't do too much wrong although I dragged some of my goal kicks away to the right, so that was something I knew I would have to work on. The nerves had disappeared when the game started but I think I was so anxious when I went to take my first kick — a conversion of a try by Doug Howlett — that the referee told me to get a move on. I was pretty happy when I saw the ball sail between the uprights and that gave me confidence for the rest of the game. That first kick is so important because, if it's successful, you know your rhythm is pretty much right. I'd scored 20 points on debut — a try, six conversions and a penalty goal — so I was able to sleep soundly, happy that I'd passed my first test.

But there's little respite when you're an All Black. From Hamilton we went to Christchurch for the next test, against France the following Saturday, and again I was named to start at second five-eighth.

Playing a test in your hometown is easier than playing anywhere else. Everything is familiar and if you want to get out of the team's hotel, just to get away for a while, there's always someone to go and have a chat with. Another difference in preparing for this test, compared with Wales in Hamilton, was that this was France. They're a hard team to prepare for because they chop and change their players round more than just about any other international side and also because once you're on the park, it's difficult to predict what they're likely to do.

If we're playing Australia or South Africa or some other side, we generally know how they're going to play in any given circumstances. We know the strengths and weaknesses of their players, just as they know ours I suppose. But with France it's different and it's therefore more important to concentrate on your own game. The French arrived in Christchurch from Buenos Aires, where they had lost to Argentina on successive weekends. They also named a team several places different from what we would have expected for a first-choice lineup. But the wise heads who guided the All Blacks were not fooled for a minute. This was France. Expect the unexpected.

During the week I watched the tape of the Welsh match and I had a few chats with Robbie Deans about my game so I was reasonably happy leading into the French game, with just the qualification that of all teams, they could spring a few surprises. There was still the need to think about my own game and, of course, I was still very much in a learning mode, watching and listening to the more senior All Blacks as they went about their routines.

It was a strange game in some ways. Everything seemed to go right for the All Blacks in the early stages and after half an hour, Joe Rokocoko had scored three tries and we were 19–6 up. But then the French forwards began to exert a bit more control and the

Opposite page: With All Blacks assistant coach Robbie Deans during the 2003 international season.

possession we had been getting dried up a bit. The match became much more of a contest and, while I don't think we were ever in any real danger of losing, we certainly didn't have total dominance and didn't win by the large margin that looked possible in the early stages. We won 31–23 in the end and fortunately we were helped by some French infringements, and the rhythm I'd had with my goalkicking in Hamilton hadn't deserted me.

The French test was another lesson along the way for me. Every match is different and something can be learnt from each one. I also learnt that whoever the opponent might be, there's no such thing as an easy test for the All Blacks.

John Mitchell named a new squad for the Tri-nations and I was gratified to see that I was still in it. No All Black, no matter who or how experienced, takes his selection for granted. That would be fatal. Even in my debut year, there were any number of players who would have been chosen by the amateur selectors but not chosen by the professional ones: Taine Randell, Christian Cullen, Byron Kelleher, Andrew Mehrtens, Scott Robertson — these among others were recent All Blacks who were not in the first two squads named for the year.

Aaron Mauger had been injured during the first part of the season, but he returned for the Tri-nations so I was less likely to be required to play. I was on the bench for each of the Tri-nations tests and only got on the field against Australia in Sydney and by the time I arrived, the damage had been well and truly done. The All Blacks had beaten South Africa in Pretoria 52–16 — an almost unimaginable score against the Springboks — and followed that form up with a 50–21 thumping of Australia in Sydney. I got on with 20 minutes to go, taking over from Carlos Spencer at first five-eighth. I scored a try soon after my arrival and that took the score out to 38–11, so although the Australians were still competitive — and when are they not? — we had the game nicely wrapped up.

The important thing for me during the Tri-nations was just continuing to learn and soak up the atmosphere of the All Blacks camp and, of course, continuing to train with the team as well as work on the individual aspects of my own game. The main mission for the year was the World Cup, as if anyone needed telling. The whole focus had been on the cup almost

> **Again, there was that mixture of pride and joy and relief when I was named in the World Cup squad, but in truth I would have been disappointed had I not been.**

since the All Blacks had been beaten in the semi-final against France in 1999. Sometimes the All Blacks can get a little insulated from the mood of the general public or from what is being portrayed in and by the news media, but it was impossible to ignore the overwhelming obsession within New Zealand about the World Cup.

Again, there was that mixture of pride and joy and relief when I was named in the World Cup squad, but in truth I would have been disappointed had I not been. I was still a novice All Black but I felt I had done enough in the tests I had played to be persevered with. I don't take too much

Opposite page: Up against the French in Christchurch in 2003. The All Blacks won the test 31–23.
Overleaf: Cup debut — about to fend off an Italian defender in the All Blacks' opening match of the 2003 World Cup, which we won 70–7.

notice of what is being written about me, but I was aware that I was being increasingly described as a utility player. That was understandable since at the time I was covering two positions and I would have been happy to play anywhere just as long as I was still part of the All Blacks, but I had no yearning to be tagged forever as a utility. My time would come, I thought.

I didn't expect it to be during the World Cup though. I was a backup player, there to fill in when required and there to learn. And what a lot there was to learn. I didn't realise then how different the World Cup is from any other series of tests. The focus is entirely different and the pressure is so much greater. The hype was unbelievable as we prepared to go to Australia and I just wanted to go there and get into it.

I had more game time early in the World Cup than I thought I would get, starting at second five-eighth against Italy, Canada and Tonga. It was a great experience and I learnt a lot playing in the competition. I never expected to get the 'big' games but I did get on for the last few minutes of the quarter-final against South Africa, which we won well by 29–9 and seemed to have us heading in the right direction at the right time. I was on the bench for the semi-final against Australia and what a devastating time that was. It was shattering and, I think, it was when I first realised how the players in 1999 must have truly felt.

No one wanted to play against France in the playoff match for third and fourth — why would you when you go to the World Cup to win the gold medal? You don't go through all that preparation to win the bronze. The boys were down and it was a hard game to get ready for. But the game was still a test match, it was another opportunity to wear the black jersey and play for New Zealand and John Mitchell stayed as much as he could with his first-choice lineup to give them a chance of some sort of compensation after losing the semi-final. I replaced Aaron Mauger in about the first quarter of the match.

The whole experience of the World Cup in Australia, but especially the last week, made me want more. Playing in such a tournament was enjoyable and I wanted more for that reason, but the last week also gave me a resolve and a hunger to be in France in 2007 and to win the World Cup. I know several other players feel exactly the same way. We knew we were good enough to win in 2003, but we didn't. It's unfinished business, and we know we can do it.

Opposite page: Another fend — this time on the French replacement fullback, Nicolas Brusque, in the World Cup play-off match in 2003.

Second Year,
Second-five

The second year at the top of any sport is always said to be the hardest. In the first year, you're the new kid on the block and while there's pressure on you to perform, the expectations don't seem all that great. It's as if people — including opponents — are reserving judgment. Also, opponents don't know a lot about you so you're pretty much left to play the way you know you can because they haven't yet worked you out or planned ways to try to counter your game. The first year is a bit of a honeymoon period, I suppose, a year of grace. The pressure you're under generally is what you impose on yourself.

But the second year is an altogether different story. For a start, you know yourself that it will be harder so therefore you have to work harder over the summer — or what summer is left to a professional footballer — on the various aspects of your game. Your team-mates will expect more of you and opponents start taking greater notice because they're more familiar with your game. I was conscious of these things after the World Cup in 2003 and as I prepared for 2004.

I spent as much time as I could in the gym and working on the various aspects of my game, though I was a little hampered by a bit of a knee injury that I'd picked up at the World Cup. It meant I couldn't do as much physically as I would have liked, but I was able to spend more time studying videos of my play and working out what I could have done better or what I should have done and I also took the opponent's view — if I came up against myself, how would I react in this or that situation. It was just constant focus on the season ahead.

I was resigned to continuing as second five-eighth, although I don't think 'resigned' is the word. I was content to be at second-five as long as that meant I was playing and I started to think of myself as a second-five, though there seemed to be an increasing number of people asking me which position I preferred: first or second. Doesn't worry me mate, as long as I'm playing.

The Crusaders had Andrew Mehrtens of course and during the 2004 Super 12, Aaron Mauger and Cameron McIntyre also played in the No 10 jersey, with me outside in each game in the No 12. The important thing was that I enjoyed the Crusaders environment — they're a great bunch of guys and the way we get on with each other and complement each other's play is, I think, one of the big factors in the success the team has enjoyed. Whatever position I was in, I knew that the life of a professional footballer was the one for me.

Every season is different and presents new challenges. There's the old rugby cliché about taking each game as it comes and I suppose the reason it's a cliché is that it is just so true. The minute you start thinking ahead beyond the next game is the minute you could get tripped up. Every game is a challenge and, especially for someone as inexperienced as me, has the potential to thrust me in a position I haven't been in before. Preparation is just so important.

Opposite page: Running up the Port Hills near Godley Head during a Crusaders pre-season workout in 2004.

We dropped the first two games in the 2004 Super 12 to the Waratahs and the Blues but then picked up a few wins before we headed for South Africa. That trip became crucial for our season. If we didn't pick up points there, we'd be in danger of missing the semi-finals and being in the top four is always the first of the Crusaders' collective goals. Even though all the players are now well used to it, the South African trip is never easy. The best part of 24 hours is spent getting there and that's a long time for fit sportsmen to be cooped up in an aeroplane — a long time for anyone, really. Jet lag is a real factor and then you have to confront South African teams on their own grounds in front of their own partisan supporters. If people think crowds at Jade or Waikato Stadium are one-eyed for the Crusaders or the Chiefs, they ought to go to a game in South Africa. There, you really experience what partisan crowds are like.

We lost to the Sharks in Durban which made the second game, against the Cats in Johannesburg, that much more vital. Ellis Park does not turn a friendly face toward visitors, but that was where we had to win. It's a game that has stuck in my memory because it was such an unusual game in that we played well and built up a big lead, a lead that any reasonable person would have thought unassailable. We were up 29–6 at halftime then up by more than 30 early in the second half. Then the game changed for no apparent reason and they started piling on the points — in fact, they became the first team in the Super 12 to turn around a 30-point deficit. It wasn't as if we started playing badly all of a sudden. It was just that South African teams can be so dangerous when things start going their way. They get a roll on, the crowd gets in behind them and makes an awful racket and they seem to grow in stature as well as in confidence. They took the lead — a lead they should never have had — not long before the finish and the siren sounded when they were up by a point. Then the referee, Matt Goddard of Australia, found one of them offside and as soon as I saw his arm go out for advantage, I knew the pressure would come on me. But that's what I train and prepare for. I was nervous — who wouldn't be? — but one of my jobs in the team was to kick the goals and that's what I had to do. I thrive on that sort of pressure. Of course the crowd bayed and booed but it's possible to shut all of that

Opposite page: Playing for the Crusaders in a pre-season match against the Queensland Reds in Timaru in 2004. The Reds won 54–38.

Ellis Park in Johannesburg in 2004, when the Crusaders just held off an incredible comeback by the Cats.
Right: Fending off Cats lock Gerrie Britz.
Above: The siren has sounded and I've kicked the penalty goal that gives us a 39–37 win.

out and just concentrate on the job in hand. It wasn't an especially difficult kick; about 15 metres in from touch and just out from the 22. I just told myself to think of the routine I'd been through hundreds of times before, don't change anything, don't think of anything else, and everything would be sweet. And it was. We won by two points. It was only later I saw when I studied the game on video that when I was in the act of kicking, one of their players threw his headgear and it landed about a metre away from me. I didn't notice it at the time and I don't think it was picked up by the live television coverage. It was just through studying different angles on the video that I noticed it. I guess that shows two things: one that my concentration was as it should have been and, secondly, that South Africans will let no chance go by to put you off.

I was proud of the way we fought back even though the chances of winning looked increasingly unlikely.

That win against the Cats was critical, as it turned out, because we achieved a home semi-final despite a last-round loss to the Hurricanes in Wellington. We beat the Stormers in the semi at Jade and then had to go to Canberra for the final. That was the game in which the Brumbies threw everything at us from the whistle and we had no answer. It was probably their best performance of the year and what better way for a rugby team than to save their best for the final? Within 20 minutes, they were up 33–0. They have such talented players and everything went well for them. We didn't give up — that's not the Crusaders way — and I was proud of the way we fought back even though the chances of winning looked increasingly unlikely. Cameron McIntyre had started the game at first five-eighth but Robbie Deans put Andrew Mehrtens on in the first half. Mehrtens, who hadn't had much game time in the Super 12, was in great form. We managed to get the score to a respectable 38–47.

A week or so later, with a new All Blacks selection panel of Graham Henry, Steve Hansen, Wayne Smith and Sir Brian Lochore, I played in my first All Blacks trial. Trials are strange sorts of games. For a start, both teams were at the Rugby Institute in Palmerston North for a few days leading up to the game and it was full-on from morning till night. I was

Super semi: Evading a Stormers tackle in the Super 12 semi-final in Christchurch in 2004.

Canberra final — trying to get away from Stirling Mortlock in the final, which was won by the Brumbies. Owen Finegan is there to lend a hand.

in the Probables team, which was pretty much a shadow All Blacks test XV and we knew the other team, the Possibles, would be doing everything possible to upset us, and why wouldn't they? Team-mates one week, but opponents the next. In the Possibles were two of my Crusaders team-mates, Aaron Mauger and Caleb Ralph, and there was no reason to expect they would be any less competitive than when they wore red and black.

A trial is a bit difficult to prepare for. You're thrust into a scratch team and there's an awful lot of game organisation to cram into a few days. There's no background, no heritage to call on, no talk of what we might have done wrong the previous week — or done right — and what we could improve on. It's also a combination, if unspoken, of team and individual performance. Every individual wants to shine to impress the selectors but each one also knows that the best way to shine is to do the job for the team, not for himself. All the players, regardless of where they're from, know one another and many have been team-mates in the past with various sides. And selectors know so much about players through watching them in Super 12 or NPC and then endless study of tapes.

The trial in Auckland went as we in the Probables thought it would. The Possibles, the guys who had everything to play for and nothing to lose, did throw everything at us and for a time looked as if they might pull off a win, which might have upset a few calculations and predictions. But we got there in the end and it was every bit as hard as we thought it would be.

It was a relief for it to be over and to be named in the first All Blacks team of the year, the first All Blacks team of the Henry era. I was once again at second five-eighth outside of Carlos Spencer. Just one final word about the trial; in the All Blacks team on the blindside of the scrum was Jono Gibbes, who had captained the Possibles team at Eden Park. So there was proof that someone could play his way into the All Blacks from the trial. Nick Evans and Sam Tuitupou had also been in the Possibles team and made their debuts in the first test of the year.

There was a great sense of expectation and excitement when we got together for the first test because it was against England, the winners of the World Cup the year before and we were determined to do well. The match was billed as the match that should have been the

Opposite page: Trials are difficult matches for which to prepare. Waiting for duty in Auckland in 2004 with Tana Umaga.

The 'new teachers' — Graham Henry, Steve Hansen and Wayne Smith.

World Cup final, but we didn't think like that. We just wanted to play well against the team that held the World Cup. That first week was a bit like arriving at school with new teachers — Graham Henry, Steve Hansen and Wayne Smith were the new teachers and the players were the pupils trying to impress.

There were quite a few new faces among the players and, with new coaches, there was a lot of work to be done, more than normal before a test match. It's necessary to go over team patterns and calls and all that sort of game stuff, but there were also a lot of peripheral things to do that are part and parcel of being an All Black, especially with the first team of the year. Though Smith and Hansen had a strong association with Canterbury, I hadn't been coached by either of them and in fact had had very little to do with them or with Henry. But it was a comfortable camp because one of the key factors with the three of them was that they were easy to get on with and with each of them, there was no doubt about what was required.

There wasn't any talk within the All Blacks about any possibility of my becoming the first five-eighth, and why should there have been with two world-class first-fives, Carlos Spencer and Andrew Mehrtens, also in the squad? I was there as second-five and that was where I was happy to be.

As I said, we were anxious to do well in that first test in Dunedin because it was the first test of a new era and also because it was against England, a team the All Blacks love to beat, World Cup or not. We didn't regard it as their cup team anyway, because they were without their cup captain, Martin Johnson, who had retired, and without several of the key cup players, including Wilkinson. It didn't matter to us who was in their team — the only thing that mattered was that the players opposing us were wearing the white jersey of England.

We achieved everything we wanted to in that test at Carisbrook and, with hindsight, it was probably the best performance of the year. Joe Rokocoko set the tone with a scything run early on during which Englishmen tried in vain to tackle him. As always, it was the forwards who provided our platform for success and they gained all the possession we needed. England seemed to struggle to come to terms with our game, which was based on attack and counter-attack, and it was only late in the match, when we knew it was secure, that England tried some serious attacking of their own. England were well beaten, as even their coach, Clive Woodward, said later. With such a dream run from the players in front of me, I had a troublefree game and came away happy with what I'd been able to achieve. I even got a 10-minute rest, Sam Tuitupou replacing me with 10 minutes to go.

People sometimes ask me how difficult it is to prepare for the next test when you've just won so well. After a loss or even just a poor winning performance, what's needed before the next test is obvious. There are clearly areas of the game which require a lot of work. It's true you learn more from losses than from wins, but we had no trouble becoming motivated for the second test in Auckland the following week. It was still England, after all, and we felt that their pride would demand a much stronger performance so we had to be doubly aware of the dangers they could present. We were also conscious that All Blacks history shows — and even our own recent history — that we don't often put together consecutive efforts of the best class.

Overleaf: On the way to a try at Eden Park in the second test against England in 2004. The England defender is wing Tom Voyce.

So it proved in Auckland. England began much better than they had in Dunedin and perhaps we might have been tested more than we were, but they lost a lot of momentum when their lock, Simon Shaw, was sent off for kneeing Keith Robinson in the back. At this level of rugby, 14 men should never seriously challenge 15. The game had a lot of intensity in it. There were some reservations about the way we played in that second test, or the way in which we had been allowed to play, but the bottom line was that in two tests, we had scored 72 points and they had scored 15. That to me was a pretty persuasive argument.

Although I was only in my second year in the All Blacks, I had lost a lot of the shyness and first-day-at-school feeling that I'd had the year before. This was due more to the fact there were a number of players newer than me now, rather than any blooming of confidence on my part. I think too that I had become a fairly settled member of the team

. . . only a fool would ever take an All Blacks start for granted.

— though only a fool would ever take an All Blacks start for granted — and that helped my confidence and self-belief. It meant that all the training and preparation I was doing was paying off; that I was doing the jobs asked of me to the satisfaction of the selectors and of myself.

I missed the next test of the year, against Argentina in Hamilton, when Sam Tuitupou started at second five-eighth, but I was back for the next, against the Pacific Islands. That was a bit of a novelty because they were a new team, had played pretty well in their earlier matches in Australia, and we had never played them, even though we had personal knowledge of many of their players (and some of them would soon be All Blacks as well). Preparations for test matches such as these can sometimes be different because with the best will in the world, subconsciously you know they're not going to be the threat that any of the big four, Australia, South Africa, France and England, will be. But it is still a test match and while the buildup may start off low-key early in the week, by the Friday it doesn't matter who the opponents are; it's still a test match and you're still wearing the All Blacks jersey. There is also the factor for me personally, and I suspect for other All Blacks

Opposite page: Caught during the test against the Pacific Islands at Albany in 2004.

too, that regardless of who the opponent is, you concentrate on your own game during the week, working on things you know need working on, or thinking about things that you know require thought. Whether I'm playing Australia or whoever, my yardstick is still my own game, not what the opponents may or may not do.

The Pacific Islanders were adventurous and scored some good tries, but we did too and of course we had a couple of Pacific Islanders of our own and it may be a bit of an irony that in a New Zealand test match against the Pacific Islands, two of our tries were scored by a Fijian, Joe Rokocoko, and two of theirs were scored by Sitiveni Sivivatu, who would become an All Black not too much later.

If you think my rugby life has just been one dream ride to the top, think again. The Tri-nations of 2004 did not leave me with particularly happy memories. The first test, against Australia in Wellington, was played in shocking conditions. It was very wet and there was some wind and I can just imagine what it would have been like if the test had been played at Wellington's earlier test venue, Athletic Park. At least at the Westpac Stadium there is some protection from the wind, but none from the rain. As usual in weather like that, the team that

The big wet. Kicking for goal in the rain during the All Blacks' 16–7 win against Australia in Wellington in 2004.

Trying to evade South African prop Eddie Andrews in the Tri-nations test in Christchurch, won 23–21 by New Zealand.

better adapts to the conditions is generally the team that will win. I think we did adapt better than the Wallabies, which is not to say that we enjoyed the conditions any more. It's a good indication of how bad the conditions were that it was only 3–0 at halftime, an almost unheard-of scoreline in modern rugby. We scored a bit more in the second half but the Wallabies, who never know when they are beaten, came back at us and we knew we had to work very hard for the 16–7 win, which meant that the Bledisloe Cup stayed in New Zealand.

We then played South Africa in Christchurch and we just got away with a win there, Doug Howlett scoring in the last seconds of the match and securing the win. It wasn't a very convincing performance by us and we knew it was a far cry from the top effort of the first win against England or the authority of the second. My Tri-nations came to an end in the next match, against Australia in Sydney. I twisted an ankle during the first half and though I tried to continue, I knew it was fruitless and I was potentially damaging the team's chances so I left the field just after halftime. It didn't help my state of mind that the All Blacks lost. There's no worse place to be than the All Blacks' dressing room after a loss. We know what losing means not just to the All Blacks, but to the whole country. It's not a pleasant feeling.

I still went to South Africa for the Tri-nations finale but there was never any realistic chance of me playing. You just do what you can in those circumstances to help the rest of the team, even if a lot of the time you just feel like a spare part. I can sympathise with those players who were injured on long tours and couldn't play; I can just imagine the way they felt, as if they were just tourists sponging off their team-mates' endeavours. I watched the test from the stand at Ellis Park and didn't enjoy it one bit. I'm not a fan at the best of times of sitting in a stand watching, but it was made even more galling this time because the All Blacks lost again, the South Africans riding on the back of their noisy crowd support and fulfilling the promise they had shown in Christchurch. So the Tri-nations was won by South Africa and we were third in a three-horse race; not a very satisfactory end to the international season that had begun so well against England. But we would be back. That's what losing does to an All Black — deepens the determination to win next time.

Overleaf: Lining up a shot at goal while Tana Umaga rallies the boys during the loss to Australia in Sydney in 2004.

I was over my ankle injury in time to play for Canterbury in the NPC and the first task was a Ranfurly Shield challenge against Bay of Plenty in Mt Maunganui. I can easily understand how an older generation had such a passion for the shield and how some of them think that shield rugby is not what it used to be. Let me say that players of my generation love playing for the shield and, even better, love winning it. I'm absolutely sure that the shield has lost none of its attraction for the modern player. We went to Mt Maunganui knowing that NPC points were on offer but, more importantly, we knew how valuable the shield was — not just for Canterbury rugby, but for Christchurch and the province in general. As far as I'm concerned, the shield still means an awful lot. I know we were thrilled to win it and it was a pleasure to be able to accompany it back to Christchurch.

Aussie McLean was keen to keep Andrew Mehrtens, Aaron Mauger and me all in the lineup, so he moved me out a place.

By this time, I had found myself a new position — at centre. The Canterbury coach, Aussie McLean, was keen to keep Andrew Mehrtens, Aaron Mauger and me all in the lineup, so he moved me out a place. I wasn't always comfortable there and tended to creep in a little and the second match, against Taranaki, was probably one of my worst games and, to make it even worse, we lost. Aussie thought that perhaps Aaron and I in the midfield weren't big enough so he remedied that by bringing Casey Laulala back into centre and plonking me at fullback — another new experience! I must say it took me a few games to get used to it — it's a pretty lonely position. I had two games at fullback, then two at second-five, then the last two at fullback again, including the NPC final win against Wellington. By the end of that, I felt more comfortable there but that was the end of the experimenting. A whole new career was about to open up for me.

No sooner was the NPC final over than the All Blacks selectors named their squad for a European tour with tests against Italy, Wales and France. As always, I was relieved to be

Opposite page: Making a break for Canterbury in the NPC final in Wellington in 2004. We won the match 40–27.

named in the squad. Before we even left New Zealand, the selectors had planned ahead and knew pretty much who would be playing in which games. I was taken aside and told that I would be at first five-eighth against Italy and whatever happened after that would be up to me. Carlos Spencer and Andrew Mehrtens were not on the tour, but other possibles for the No 10 jersey were Aaron Mauger and Luke McAlister. It was up to me. I was pleased but knew it was a heavier responsibility than I had been used to because the first-five calls the tactical shots. Rather than just thinking about my own game, I had to think about others around me as well — I had to give the tactical direction rather than follow. It meant my preparation was more intense than ever and I had to do a lot more homework; analysing moves on the video and doing other things to the point at which it became instinctive — no time to think. It helped that there were more new guys in the team and that I felt more confident about speaking up from my lofty 'senior' position!

Caught in the 2004 test against Italy. Steven Bates moves in to help.

I suppose it was good to start in Rome because, meaning no disrespect, the Italian game did not have the same intensity as those in Cardiff or Paris. It was a good game in which to become accustomed to my new role and I was happy enough with the way it went, especially when it was a 59–10 win for the All Blacks. On the strength of that, I was first five-eighth for the rest of the short tour providing I didn't make a very large mess of things. The second game, against Wales, was my first appearance at Millennium Stadium and what an experience. Like every New Zealander, I'd heard all about the singing in Cardiff and about the intensity and passion of the Welsh people for rugby. I've played in front of noisy crowds — they don't get much noisier than Loftus in Pretoria — but I don't think I was prepared for Cardiff. I can see how some players may have been intimidated by it but equally, some players draw strength from it. I'm told the crowds in Cardiff don't sing as much as they used to — all I can say is that they must have been terribly noisy before.

Assisting Richie McCaw in the 2004 test against Wales, won by a single point by the All Blacks.

There were times during the test in 2004 I couldn't hear the calls and we had to slow things down because communication was so difficult. Of course it helped the Welsh crowd that their team played pretty well that day and could have beaten us for the first time in 50 years — remember we won only by a point. The noise of the Cardiff crowd is in direct relation to the performance of the Welsh team. That was why it was so noisy. I'm not saying the noise upset the way we played, but I'm sure it affected the way the Welsh played. They thrived on it and good on them; we didn't play as well as we knew we could and they sniffed a chance for a victory that, if achieved, they'd still be celebrating. I certainly wouldn't have liked being a part of the first All Blacks team to lose to Wales since 1953, and it was close. They provided a whole set of challenges for the All Blacks and for me in particular — the way their defence came up so suddenly was a good, and quick, lesson for me. And it was good that it was testing me; it was teaching me new aspects of the game from which I could learn. But it was a relief to come away from Cardiff with the win.

The big test of the tour was always going to be France. We knew we'd be up for a special challenge. Even before the game at the Stade de France, it was challenging. The kickoff time was 9.30 — the latest the All Blacks have ever begun a match. That means a very long day to build up, and different routines to adapt to. It may not sound much, but when all your nervous energy is geared toward the game, it's a long time to wait around. One of the great advantages for us heading into the game was Dave Gallaher, the captain of the Original All Blacks in 1905 and the leader in the first test against France. The trophy for which we played was named in his honour and the French respected him as well, because he had been killed in World War I. Of course few of the players knew much about Gallaher so Anton Oliver was given the job of briefing us and he did it superbly. He told us about Gallaher's life as an All Black, how he'd then been an All Blacks selector and how, at the age of 42, he enlisted to fight in World War I when there was no requirement for him to do so. He told us how he was killed at Passchendaele and he told us, too, of the 12 other All Blacks who were killed fighting for their country. To illustrate his point, Anton had 13 of our All Blacks stand up, each one representing a player who had died; each one about the same age

Opposite page: A special win in a special challenge. Me with the Dave Gallaher Cup after the 45–6 win against France in Paris in 2004.

as we were, each one far from home and family and friends, each one representing New Zealand on a far more deadly field of battle. It was a moving moment and made us proud to be New Zealanders and proud of what New Zealanders before us had done for their country. The least we could do was to win a rugby match for our country — and this we did in the most emphatic way possible. The French were just overwhelmed; I think they fancied their chances before the game but I'm pretty sure they knew they had no chance soon after it began. Seldom, if ever, can a French team have been as thoroughly beaten. This was the game which for a time was reduced to Golden Oldies scrums because the French forwards had taken such a pounding. The All Blacks began the year with a top performance in beating England. We ended it with an even better one against France.

There were two thoughts I had when we flew home. One was that we had set the standard for the future of All Blacks rugby; we had established a higher benchmark. The other was that as far as I was concerned, I wanted to be a part of that future — and at first five-eighth.

Year of the Lion

This was the year of the Lions. Everyone knew it — how could you not? Everyone talked about it and as for the players, well, everyone wanted to be a part of it. The Lions are rare opposition. Some great New Zealand players have gone through their distinguished careers without having played against the Lions. We were grateful for the opportunity and, for those of us chosen, the privilege.

But it never pays to look too far ahead in rugby, so first it was the Super 12 again and we started 2005 where we had left off in 2004 — at Bruce Stadium in Canberra playing against the Brumbies. They fielded all their usual suspects and again, they were fired up and, again, we came away the losers. I was at fullback because Leon MacDonald was still on his way back from Japan and Ben Blair had gone to the Highlanders in the draft. I didn't have my best night in a Crusaders jersey — or any jersey, come to that. I missed a few kicks and generally had a dreadful game. It wasn't one I look back on fondly.

The loss meant we were criticised for starting slowly, as we supposedly do every year. All I can say is that it's not by design. We obviously try to win every game, as I'm sure every team does, but seeking perfection in rugby is a far cry from actually achieving it. We couldn't have been too bad, though, because the only other game we lost in the round-robin was to the Bulls in that place New Zealand players dread, Loftus in Pretoria. I'd only had the Brumbies game at fullback, playing at first or second five-eighth in all the others, but by the time we got back to Christchurch after South Africa, I was left on the bench to play the Cats. Robbie Deans had a good reason for that. It was Justin Marshall's 100th Super 12 game and Robbie wanted to pay due tribute to him by having Andrew Mehrtens outside him. It was a nice gesture and was appreciated by all the players because 'Marshy' had been such an inspiration to all of us.

We played the Hurricanes twice in a row at Jade in 2005, the first in the last game of the round-robin, for which I was rested, then in the semi-final the following week. The rest must have done me good because I had a reasonable game, scored 22 points and, more importantly, we had a strong win, propelling us into a home final the following week against the Waratahs. Some of the other Crusaders had been Super 12 champions before but I'd been twice to the well and come away with nothing. So winning the final, and by playing good footy, was a big relief to me. I now knew how true the phrase 'third time lucky' was. It was a great way to farewell players such as Marshall, Mehrtens, Norm Maxwell, Dave Hewett and Sam Broomhall.

The Super 12 having reached a very satisfactory conclusion as far as the Crusaders were concerned, it was now time to concentrate on the international part of the season and,

Opposite page: Caught in the Super 12 semi-final against the Hurricanes in 2005, a match the Crusaders won 47–7.

Title No 5.
Right: Breaking against the Waratahs in
the Super 12 final in 2004, won 35–25
by the Crusaders.
Top: Giving 'Marshy' a congratulatory hug
in his last game for the Crusaders.
Above: Aaron Mauger and I show our
appreciation to the Crusaders supporters.

though the first test of the year was against Fiji, that really meant the Lions. The huge Lions squad was already in New Zealand and they had played Bay of Plenty and Taranaki before our first test. They were playing the Maori the night after the Fiji test and that meant the Maori had first call on any All Blacks.

I mean no disrespect when I say that Fiji were an ideal buildup game for us. It was still a test match, and still a chance to wear the All Black jersey, but no one was under any illusions that it was anything but a prelude match. We knew pretty much how they would play; they generally attack with gusto early on and they can use some unorthodox moves, but we always knew that we had too much firepower and organisation for them, even though we had six All Blacks making their debut that night. To win 91–0 was a very satisfying way to begin the international year — not that I had a lot to do with it; I was taken off at halftime when we were 50–0 up.

Now we could concentrate solely on the Lions. Even when we'd been in Europe the year before, all the talk had been about the Lions and there seemed to be an expectation — or at least a lot of hope — that the Lions under Clive Woodward would beat the All Blacks in a series for the first time since 1971. Even though the levels of anticipation were high, I wonder how many people really realised how big the Lions tour would be. I don't think any of the All Blacks really appreciated what an increase in intensity the series represented until it actually happened.

The first test was in Christchurch and, as usual, we stayed at The Heritage in the Square. From the hotel, all you could see was a sea of red — Lions supporters everywhere. It brought home to me how big the tour really was. Everything was up a level — the intensity, the anticipation, the hype. We even had security guards at our hotel, which is not a very common thing for the All Blacks, especially in New Zealand.

I'd kept an eye on the Lions in their first two or three games but concentrated more on what I had to do rather than what any of my opponents might do. I'd been looking forward to playing against Jonny Wilkinson, but he was named at second five-eighth. In the No 10 jersey was the Welshman, Stephen Jones, who had had a great Six Nations, but in the end it didn't really make much difference who was opposite me. I still had my job to do and if I did it, and if all the players felt the same way, the result would take care of itself. I know the news media talks about Carter lining up against Jones or whoever, but it's not often at first five-eighth you're in direct competition with your opposite; it's not like at halfback, for example.

The test being in Christchurch meant that I could slip home if I needed to get away from the hype. That's always a handy safety valve because while it's important to focus on the match, it's equally important not to get too wound up about it.

I'd begun keeping a diary and in it I noted things such as moves, calls, goals and little motivational messages to myself. Nothing very deep. Just odd words that I would glance at and say to myself as a reinforcement. During the Lions series, I jotted down words such as 'relax' and 'work rate' as reminders. The coaches had suggested that keeping such diaries might be a good idea and several of the players did it.

Opposite page: Attacking against Fiji in the opening test of 2005 at Albany.

Above: Chris Jack, Carl Hayman, Richie McCaw, Doug Howlett and me during the national anthem before the first Lions test in 2005. Opposite: A break in play during the 21–3 win.

The abiding thought during that week in Christchurch was just for the game to happen. There was such a buildup it seemed to take an age in coming. I'm told there hadn't been a buildup to a test series like it for years. Some said not since the last Lions in 1993, others not since the World Cup final in 1987. The Lions had lost only to the Maori in their tour games and while they had not been all that convincing, there was the thought that all would come right for them in the test. On the old tours, I'm told, teams could play stinkers in the midweek matches but then play like world-beaters in the tests. So, perhaps, the Lions.

But not this time. The conditions at Jade were shocking — wind and rain and a temperature that hovered round zero. At halftime, I rushed into the dressing room and held my hands under the hot water to get some feeling back into them. The All Blacks adapted well to the conditions, certainly better than the Lions, and we gained early on the forward domination we needed. The conditions pretty much dictated that it would be a fairly tight, low-scoring game and the margin of our win, 21–3, was commanding by

those standards. Two tries to none was an ample answer to all the Lions fans whose chants echoed around Jade.

It was a great feeling to win the first test, and the boys were relieved in the dressing room afterwards, but we knew one win did not win a series. The all-important match was on the following Saturday; only then could we relax if we won. We suspected too that the Lions, having been so exposed in Christchurch, would be a tougher proposition in Wellington.

It was another test week but with greater intensity because of all the talk about the Lions and of all the public interest. In Wellington, we stayed in the City Life Apartments. They're off Lambton Quay and therefore in the centre of the city, but they're secluded and not like a hotel where people wander in and out all the time. It was an ideal place in which to prepare. We trained at Rugby League Park and I had a few kicks at Westpac Stadium on the Friday and generally did what I always do — just remind myself about things I have to do and go through all my normal preparations. There were special aspects to the test, but nothing special as far as I was concerned personally. It was another test for which I had to prepare as thoroughly as possible.

All Blacks v Lions, Second Test

By Ron Palenski

Wellington turns on a sparkling night for the second test. The stadium is packed with the red of Lions supporters seemingly outnumbering the black. The anticipation and tension is almost tangible. The roar of 'Lions, Lions, Lions' as Gareth Thomas leads his troops onto the field, then the less unified but still loud roar as Wellington's favourite son, Tana Umaga, leads the All Blacks on. Clive Woodward, the most talked about of the Lions party, had made 11 changes from the first test. Among them, Jonny Wilkinson is at first five-eighth and Thomas, the Welsh fullback and new captain, is at centre.

The All Blacks, too, had made changes. Byron Kelleher is at halfback in place of Justin Marshall, Mils Muliaina is back at fullback instead of Leon MacDonald, Rico Gear is on the right wing instead of Doug Howlett and in the pack, Greg Somerville replaces Carl Hayman, who has an infected toe.

When the players line up for the anthems, Dan Carter stands between his Canterbury and Crusaders team-mates, Chris Jack and Aaron Mauger, an arm round each. To complete the Christchurch symmetry, Hayley Westenra sings the national anthem.

It is almost possible to detect the intensity of the fire in Umaga's eyes as he stands his ground ahead of his team-mates during the haka. This is not just another test match. This is utu. This is payback time for a week of damnation from the mouths of Woodward and O'Driscoll.

As Umaga, Gear and Mauger lead the haka, the Lions stand and watch, their tracksuits still on. The Lions supporters do their best to drown out the haka with another chant of 'Lions! Lions! Lions!' That could obscure the sound, but makes not one blind bit of difference to the intensity of feeling in the hearts and minds of the All Blacks.

The pre-match rituals over, Australian referee Andrew Cole signals time on and Wilkinson, to another roar from the crowd, kicks off to his right. Richie McCaw is underneath it but the ball bounces forward off a shoulder. Cole sees it as a knock-on. The Lions halfback, Dwayne Peel, goes left from the scrum and from the set-up, Wilkinson goes left again and passes to Thomas. His eyes must light up because he cuts inside Jack

The All Blacks lay down the challenge to the Lions in the second test in Wellington.

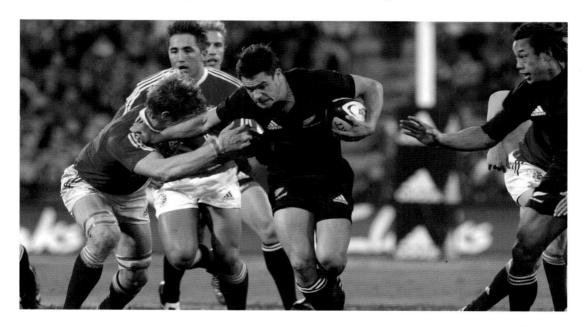

Trying to break clear of Lewis Moody during the second test. Gavin Henson is ready to help Moody and Tana Umaga is there for me.
Overleaf: Breaking the line with Tana Umaga and Sitiveni Sivivatu in support. Lions centre Gavin Henson is chasing.

and Keven Mealamu and there are no other All Black defenders there. He scores under the crossbar and Wilkinson converts. 7–0.

Carter kicks off to the left and the ball is taken by the Lions No 8, Ryan Jones. He gets it back to Peel, who finds a gap around the fringes and hares off upfield. He finds Thomas to his right but is dragged down. Cole fingers an All Black for playing the ball on the ground in the ensuing ruck. Wilkinson's kick at goal goes outside the left upright.

The Lions attack from the dropout and have control of the ball in a ruck just a few metres out from the All Blacks' line. The Irish lock, Paul O'Connell, charges in and swallow dives over the ruck. Coles says it's silly and Carter kicks the defensive penalty to touch.

Six minutes have gone and the All Blacks get their first throw into a lineout. Keven Mealamu finds Chris Jack and he taps the ball down to Justin Collins. The ball goes to Carter and he kicks deep into Lions territory. Josh Lewsey, the Lions fullback, kicks it back but doesn't get great distance. There's a ruck and one of the Lions is penalised for entering from the side. Carter's first kick at goal for the night, this one from 35 metres, is true. 7–3.

The minutes tick by, the match moving at a frenetic pace. The Lions attack more than they could in Christchurch, but the All Blacks keep their composure. The Lions win a lineout against the throw but can't clear. The scrum has to be reset and the All Blacks win possession. Carter kicks and lands the ball just within the field of play. Jason Robinson does well to control it. There's a Lions knock-on and the All Blacks go right from the scrum, Muliaina then Gear to the corner but Gear is pushed into touch.

The All Blacks, with more consistent possession, attack left and right with Collins prominent. Sitiveni Sivivatu is close to going over and in the ruck, Steve Thompson is penalised for going in from the side. Carter inside the 22 and almost straight in front kicks the goal. 7–6.

The Lions win lineout ball and Thomas charges into the midfield. The ball is knocked from his grasp by Mauger's tackle and Umaga flicks it up to Mauger, who passes on to Carter. He runs left, clapping on the pace past Gavin Hensen and round Shane Williams. When Lewsey comes across, Carter passes inside to Umaga and he scores. There could be no more appropriate first try-scorer for the All Blacks. Carter converts. 13–7.

Opposite page: Second test against the Lions. It was a good day for me with the boot — nine out of ten.

The Lions are not done for. They attack again and again and from one of these, Wilkinson fires out a long pass to Thomas and he's held by Carter. The Lions go left from the breakdown and are held 10 m from the line. Mauger, thinking the ball is out, leans over the ruck to grab Peel but Cole says the ball wasn't out. Wilkinson 5 m in from touch and 23 m out kicks the goal. 13–10.

Carter responds almost immediately when O'Connell is penalised for not releasing the ball on the ground after the kickoff. Carter in front 25 m out kicks it. 16–10.

Mauger kicks deep after a missed dropped goal attempt by Wilkinson and Lewsey returns it, then recovers his own kick. An All Black is penalised in the maul and Wilkinson kicks the goal from 42 m in front. 16–13.

Just on the half-hour, the All Blacks attack twice on the blindside. Kelleher runs blind and is caught just short of the line by Thomas. The All Blacks retain possession while the Lions argue Kelleher should have been penalised for not releasing. From the scrum, Kelleher passes to Carter and he hands it on to Mauger, then doubles round to receive the ball again and passes to Gear who pops it over to Sivivatu and he slides across the line in the tackles of Lewsey and Williams. Carter's conversion from wide out is just to the left. 21–13.

Mauger has to go off with injury and there's confusion about who is replacing him. Ma'a Nonu goes on but before play resumes he's replaced by Leon MacDonald.

There's so much noise in the stadium, from the crowd and from the Lions players who seem to query every decision, that Cole has to ask one of his touch judges, Stu Dickinson, if the 'hooter' has gone. As Dickinson replies, the siren sounds.

The match organisers prove to be extraordinarily generous hosts at halftime because they allow a Welsh male voice choir onto the ground. This fires the Lions supporters up even more as 'Feed Me Till I Want No More' reverberates around the ground.

In the first minute of the second half, the All Blacks go left from the kickoff and Carter gets the ball to Umaga. The captain is tackled by Wilkinson but he stays on the ground, writhing from a shoulder injury. Julian White is penalised for being offside and Carter, from 36 m and just to the left of the posts, kicks the goal. 24–13.

Byron Kelleher makes a break from deep within All Black territory and when he's caught, the All Black forwards drive the ball on. Keven Mealamu peels away with it and

About to score the first of my two tries against the Lions in the second test.

flings a pass to Rodney So'oialo. He gets the ball to Carter who's just inside the touchline. He runs down the line then drops the ball on to his left foot and grubbers past the one remaining defender, Josh Lewsey. Carter whips past him and regathers his kick just centimetres from touch-in-goal. It's the try of the match. Carter completes his class act with the conversion from the touchline. 31–13.

The Lions are way behind on the scoreboard but they are not yet beaten. They attack from the left and from the right and only big crunching tackles by Rico Gear and Ali Williams — both of them on Shane Williams as it happens — keep them out.

The match has a greater intensity than the first test in Christchurch and is played at a terrific pace. The Lions continue to attack but the black line of defence is impregnable. Julian White is penalised in a scrum and Carter kicks the All Blacks back down into Lions territory. The All Blacks have a turn on attack and gain 40 m. Cole finds a Lions infringement and Carter kicks the goal. 34–13.

Wilkinson is still troubled by his shoulder injury and he's replaced by the first-five from the first test, Stephen Jones. It's an opportune time for the All Blacks to make changes too, and Justin Marshall goes on for Kelleher and Sione Lauaki for Collins.

The Lions gain some reward for their constant endeavour — even if it's only consolation — when Peel breaks on the blindside and is able to send his Llanelli team-mate, Simon Easterby, over in the corner. Jones's conversion attempt goes to the right. 34–18.

But the All Blacks are not finished. Neither is Carter. Gear kicks downfield and it's nicely trapped by Robinson, but he's caught before he can retaliate. Cole shouts out an advantage to black and Marshall goes to the left, gets the ball to Tony Woodcock, then to MacDonald and then to Carter who steps inside Thomas and is across the line ahead of Shane Williams. Carter again converts his own try. 41–18.

The pace of the match is taking its toll, especially among the bigger Lions forwards. Replacements stream on to the ground and the All Black coach, Graham Henry, clears his bench. Umaga kicks the All Blacks to within metres of the line and Carter takes it on, but he's caught just short and in the tackle falls on the point of a shoulder. The Lions are penalised for joining the maul from the side and McCaw snaps up the ball and drives over. Carter has his shoulder seen to then kicks the conversion and promptly leaves the field. It's 48–18.

With no replacements left, the All Blacks play the last minute or so with just 14 men, with MacDonald playing at first-five. It is an emphatic win.

Below: My second try against the Lions. Right: At this moment I don't seem to mind the shoulder injury that much.

I was on the bench when the game ended and had ice on my shoulder. We were ecstatic. We'd gained the win we wanted in the manner in which we wanted it. We'd beaten the Lions in the series. We'd taken our level of play up another step from the win in Paris the year before. We had set a new standard for the All Blacks. It was a great feeling.

In the dressing room, my phone went crazy. Ma'a Nonu and I had a competition to see who would get the most text messages. I won hands down. There must have been 50 messages, all within minutes of the end of the game. Ma'a couldn't believe it.

I'd had one of those games in which everything goes right and in which opportunities present themselves. I was content, but the happiness I felt was for the team, not for me.

> I was taken out and plonked down in front of them (journalists) but I didn't know what to say. I didn't even know how many points I'd scored and one of them had to tell me.

I don't know how many journalists were at Westpac — there must have been more than a hundred — and they all seemed to want to talk to me. I was taken out and plonked down in front of them but I didn't know what to say. I didn't even know how many points I'd scored and one of them had to tell me. I just wanted to be with the rest of the team in the dressing room — it's difficult talking to the media after the game because you want to be with your team-mates and your immediate thoughts are not about how well you played or what you did. When I was asked what I thought when I scored or what went through my mind when I got the ball, I didn't know. At that pace and at that level, you just let the instincts take over.

The decision was made fairly soon that I would not play in the third test in Auckland. Even if the series had not been sealed, I wouldn't have played. I didn't want to risk aggravating the injury and the selectors were of the same mind. I went back to Christchurch for the week then rejoined the All Blacks in Auckland later, doing what I could to support them and, in particular, my replacement, Luke McAlister. I sat in the stand and revelled in the All Blacks' success as they made it a clean sweep.

The injury took two or three weeks to be fully healed but I was never in danger of missing the Tri-nations. There was some talk that the old routine of playing against Australia and South Africa would be a bit of a let-down after the hype of the Lions, and there was something of a sense of an anti-climax, but we were determined to reclaim the Tri-nations title and it didn't take long for the motivation to reach the required levels.

The first of the Tri-nations matches was in Cape Town and I hadn't played for five weeks and felt a bit rusty, as if I needed a lesser level game before a test match. But there were no such luxuries. The Springboks played well, especially their defence, and they deserved their 22–16 win although I thought we came back well after a fairly slow start. The loss was a good lesson to us that, Lions beaters we may have been, but there were other sides well capable of beating us. There's no respite in test rugby. Euphoric win one minute, sorry loss the next.

The loss made us all the more determined when we headed for Sydney and the first game against Australia. We had to get our season back on track. And it was a good win,

Back to earth: Rodney So'oialo, Joe Rokocoko, Luke McAlister and me leave the field after the 22–16 loss to South Africa in Cape Town.

30–13, as it turned out, not that I was any great contributor to it. I didn't feel as if I played all that well. I kicked the goals I had to but still felt as if I'd been missing matches and things just didn't flow for me. It was all academic anyway after Clyde Rathbone came back on a cut after a ruck during the second half and he and I collided in the tackle, my horizontal left leg taking the brunt. I knew as soon as I landed that something was wrong but initially I thought it might have been just a bruised calf. I couldn't put any weight on the leg and got carried off and spent the rest of the game on the bench, with ice on the calf.

I went straight back to the hotel after the game and had a fairly sleepless night because of the pain. I left Sydney early the next morning for home and fortunately was put in business class where I could elevate the leg and put more ice on it. I was pretty miserable. The leg gave me a lot of pain and I had another sleepless night at home on the Sunday night before I had it x-rayed in Christchurch on the Monday. Far from being a bruised calf, the x-ray showed the fibula — the smaller of the two bones in the lower leg — had been broken. Fortunately, the break was not all the way through.

It was first thought that I would be out of rugby for eight to 12 weeks and it wasn't pleasant to be told that. It was the first time in my career that I would miss more than one game because of injury. The leg wasn't put in plaster and after a week or so, I was able to walk around a bit. I spent a lot of time in the pool making sure the muscles didn't suffer and, after a while, I was able to work out on a bike. It healed more quickly than the initial prognosis, but I didn't want to rush it and I was in two minds about when I thought I could return to play. I wanted to make sure that when I did get back on the field, I would be completely fit — there was no point playing too soon, not giving of my best and perhaps risking aggravation of the injury.

In the event, I was back in time for the NPC and Ranfurly Shield match against Auckland on October 8 — just under two months after being carried off in Sydney. I felt fine but my first kick — the kickoff — didn't go 10 metres so it wasn't a great way to come back. Otherwise, things seemed to be okay and I got through that match and the following one, a loss in a semi-final against Otago, without any problems. I wasn't back to my best, but far better to slowly work my way back in the NPC than in a test match. I don't mean the competition in the NPC

Opposite page: Time to go . . . I'm assisted from the field in Sydney in 2005 after breaking a bone in my left leg.

any disrespect — it can be tough — but the intensity of a test match is something else again.

I had done enough to show the selectors that I would be all right for the tour of the British Isles, about which there was more than the usual level of expectation. Part of that was because there was speculation the four teams we were playing, Wales, Ireland, England and Scotland, could be a more cohesive threat to us than their combined strength, the Lions, had been. It was also the centenary of the first All Blacks' tour in 1905 and, in the background, was the prospect of us becoming the first All Black team to achieve the grand slam since Graham Mourie's side in 1978.

Graham Henry and the selectors made it clear before we left New Zealand that everyone would get a game and that there were pretty much two distinct teams, which they had chosen before we left. It was about developing players for the future, and about developing a team capable of winning the World Cup in 2007. After the close shave the year before, we expected Wales to be hard and that they would feed off all the hype about the 1905 match, which — as no New Zealander should need reminding — the Welsh won 3–0. Anton Oliver, who had spoken to us the year before about the significance of Dave Gallaher, was

the history teacher again and he talked to us about 1905 and how the All Blacks then set the pattern for tours which were to follow. He told us how the All Blacks did the haka at Cardiff Arms Park before their test against Wales and how the Welsh responded by singing their anthem, 'Land of My Fathers', thus beginning the tradition of national anthems before test matches. The Welsh union knew this too and suggested that in honour of the centenary, the same order should apply so we had to do the haka first and then the crowd sang their anthem. It felt unusual, but it didn't make any difference to the way we played.

The Welsh were missing several players who would have been first choices and there's no way of knowing what difference they might have made. For all that, I felt we were dominant throughout the match and it was pressure that we were able to apply which led to their making mistakes. Far from being the close game some of us worried about, it proved to be a very conclusive 41–3 for the All Blacks and I was gratified that I was back to something like the form I had against the Lions. I didn't give the leg that had been broken a thought. I was told later that the 26 points I scored from two tries, five conversions and two penalty goals was a record for a New Zealander against Wales, beating by two the record set by another Canterbury man, Fergie McCormick, in Auckland in 1969.

It's always good to win a test match of course, and especially good to win in Cardiff because the Welsh supporters are so passionate and any All Black would hate to be in the first team to lose to Wales in more than 50 years. It was the first leg of the grand slam too, but we didn't talk about that. That was for the media to speculate about. As far as we were concerned, each test on the tour was self-contained — not part of a series — and after Wales the focus moved on to Ireland, then on to England and, finally, to Scotland.

I wasn't chosen for the Irish match and, as usual, the non-players did all they could to support those who were playing and we were delighted that the win in Dublin by 45–7 was as emphatic as that in Cardiff.

I was back in the firing line for the test against England, a match we suspected would probably be the most challenging of the four. It was my first time in a test at Twickenham —

Opposite page: Wales first five-eighth Stephen Jones watches as I pass to Tana Umaga on the cut in the grand slam test against Wales in 2005.
Overleaf: Passing to Aaron Mauger during the third of the grand slam tests, against England.

I'd been on the bench the year before for the Barbarians game — and it's a pretty impressive place, the tradition of the ground brought to life by the din that comes from the crowd, especially when they sing the national anthem or their 'second anthem', 'Swing Low, Sweet Chariot'. For all the stereotype of the stiff upper lip English, they can be very emotional and passionate, as anyone who has ever seen them gesticulating at referees knows. They started the test pretty fired up and when they scored first, through Martin Corry, we knew it would be every bit as tough as we'd thought it might be.

We gained the lead by the half-hour mark after a try by Tana Umaga, and I'd kicked a couple of penalty goals, but we were never in the position of having a comfortable lead. We did enough to keep our noses in front and, to be frank, there were times in the second half when we were only just able to hang on. That was the match in which we had three players sin-binned in the second half and that tested our defence, but we were able to hold England out. Our forwards were magnificent. You learn more from games like that than you do from big wins and while I may not have thought so at the time, it was a great experience for all of us and one that would stand us in good stead for the future. It was all part of building a team and setting new standards. From a personal point of view, I was just pleased to have been able to put the injury behind me and to play at a level I was happy with.

We won the Scottish test the following week and, finally, we could talk about — and celebrate — the grand slam. Because we'd consciously set the prospect aside during the tour, its achievement may not have had the same impact on the players as it did on our supporters. But being a member of just the second All Black team to beat the four British Isles rugby countries on the one tour is something that I'll take pride in later in my career or when I've finished playing.

I didn't have much time to reflect on our successes with my team-mates because some of us had to fly from Edinburgh to Paris next day for the International Rugby Board awards dinner. There, Graham Henry was named coach of the year, the All Blacks were team of the year and I was humbled by being named International Player of the Year.

It had been such a dream year I didn't want it to end.

Opposite page: The end of a dream year — in Paris with the IRB International Player of the Year trophy.

Dateline Buenos Aires

The 2006 rugby year couldn't have got off to a better start with the Crusaders winning the first Super 14 competition. We had a few new guys coming into the team but we gelled well together, began well and then had a bit of a wobble with a draw against the Force in Perth and then the loss to the Stormers in Cape Town. The Stormers game was the only one I didn't start though I got on soon after halftime. The draw and the loss were a sort of reality check and, fortunately, we were able to get our season back on track with a win the following week against the Bulls. That was especially pleasing because it's always difficult to win in Pretoria.

It was great to be involved in the first final of Super 14 and even better to be able to play it at home against the Hurricanes. The fog made it a strange night, though I suspect it was much worse for spectators and television viewers than it was for the players. There was a bit of fog when heading to the ground from our hotel.

It was worse when we got to Jade and it seemed to come in even more just before kickoff after we'd done our warmups out on the ground. We talked a little about it and what effect it might have on the way we played, but the only difficulty really was when the ball was in the air. The ball was also a little slippery because of the combination of fog and dew. But, as I said, it didn't have a great impact out in the middle. The important thing, as always, was to stick to our game plan and to avoid mistakes.

The fog made it a strange night, though I suspect it was much worse for spectators and television viewers than it was for the players.

The win was great and there was a little personal icing on the cake because my 221 points were a record for Super rugby, although I didn't set too much store by it because Andrew Mehrtens of course had two fewer games in 1998 when he set the previous record of 206.

The All Black squads for the first phase of the international season were named the day after the final and, as always, it was pleasing to know that I was included. I had been named in the squad for the test in Buenos Aires against Argentina, which meant I joined all the All Blacks in Auckland for preparation and commercial work, then went home again while the other squad stayed to prepare for the Ireland tests.

I kept a diary for the period involving the Argentina match:

Opposite page: A game from the mists of time — the Super 14 final at a foggy Jade.
Overleaf: In the fog — the players had the best view of what was going on.

Cheers, mate! Rico Gear and I salute each other after the Crusaders' win in the first Super 14 final.

Wednesday, June 14:

Fly to Auckland. After checking in to the Heritage Hotel, the first duty is skin-fold testing with the dietician, Glenn Kearney. That's the process of measuring fat on the body. Fortunately, I registered no change. Lunch at the Heritage, then training in the afternoon at the Waitakere Stadium, going over moves and phase play. We followed that with 15 against 15, our opposition drawn from young players in the Auckland area. The three All Black coaches, Graham Henry, Wayne Smith and Steve Hansen, supervise the session, their second for the day because the test team to play Ireland had trained in the morning. The whole squad gets together at night for dinner and entertainment by the Naked Samoans, Robbie and Dave, which gives us all a laugh. A few of us go to the team room afterwards to watch the league State of Origin match and it was a nice way to end the night with the team I support, Queensland, winning so well.

Thursday, June 15:

A team meeting and training in the morning for the Argentina-bound guys. I do a fair bit of washing in my hotel room then pack. Our flight to Buenos Aires leaves at 8.45 p.m. and we touch down at 1 p.m. the same day. I have little trouble sleeping on flights and I was able to get eight hours in. We get to our hotel in Buenos Aires, the Sheraton, at about 3 p.m. and we have a choice of going to the pool, the gym or for a walk. Most of us choose the walk and we have our first experience of the hugely wide streets of Buenos Aires and of a shopping mall. Dinner in the hotel and then bed.

Friday, June 16:

Training in the morning at which we have a few anaerobic games and, in honour of the World Cup in Germany that dominates Buenos Aires, we play a bit of soccer. It has to be said the standard is nowhere near as high as people in Argentina are used to. We also do a bit of running and ball work under the guidance of our strength and conditioning coach, Graham Lowe, who is one of five management team members with our group of 15 players. I just muck around the hotel in the afternoon and at night we all go out to dinner at a restaurant, where a great variety of food is available.

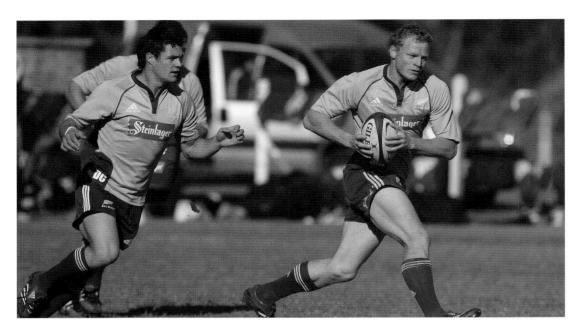

Shadowing new All Black — and Crusaders team-mate — Scott Hamilton, in training in Buenos Aires.

With Chris Masoe at training in Buenos Aires.

Saturday, June 17:

Training in the morning again. This time we do team work, patterns and fitness session. Back to the hotel for lunch and while we're eating, we're able to watch a replay of the All Blacks' win in the second test against Ireland back in Auckland. It's more test rugby after that because we go to the Velez Sarsfield Stadium to watch Argentina against Wales. The Pumas win and although the crowd is only about 15,000 they make enough noise for at least twice that. Back to the hotel for dinner and later we all go to tango dancing — to watch, I hasten to add, not to dance.

Sunday, June 18:

Today's a day off and for me, that means a lie-in. I don't do anything in the morning and then, for lunch, we all go out to a restaurant where we watch Brazil playing Australia in the World Cup. When we get back to the hotel, the rest of the party from Auckland is there to greet us. We all have dinner together and catch up with each other on what's been happening.

Monday, June 19:

Team meeting in the morning, then training, though the guys from Auckland, still overcoming the effects of the long flight, are not fully involved. We go through team playing patterns then have a recovery session in the pool. A few of us go to a mall in the afternoon then dinner in the hotel at night.

Tuesday, June 20:

Meeting again, then training. This time it's defence and Graham Henry is in charge. It's very intense and a lot of contact work, especially for those of us who have been here since Thursday. There's a lot of tackling and it's important that we get our physical conditioning back. Some haven't played a game for a while. My last was the Super 14 final three weeks before. After training, I have a kicking session with the kicking coach, Mick Byrne, in attendance. Then it's back to the hotel for pool recovery, then lunch, then a gym session in the afternoon. We go out for a team dinner at night and the entertainment committee provided a quiz. The questions had been set by the doctor, Deb Robinson. It's a whole mixture of questions. The team I was in came second.

Wednesday, June 21:

Meeting in the morning again and then training. This time it's attack training. After it, I have some food because three of us then have a fairly intensive kicking session. There's me, Luke McAlister and Piri Weepu, with Wayne Smith and Mick Byrne supervising. We do dropouts, punts and placekicks probably for about an hour and a half. Then it's back to the hotel for lunch. We go to a restaurant that night and watch Argentina playing the Netherlands in the World Cup. Back at the hotel after dinner, and I have a massage.

Thursday, June 22:

Training again in the morning, but this time it's on a surface like a hockey turf rather than a soft, muddy rugby ground. It's easier on the legs and allows us to be more explosive. I just rest in the afternoon then have some stretching exercises with the physiotherapist, Peter Gallagher. Byron Kelleher is in charge of the entertainment committee and he has organised five teams within the team — management, the Receders, the Scruffies, the Wogs and the Greasy Hairdos. I am in the Greasy Hairdos. We are each sent to a different restaurant and the Hairdos go Japanese — that works out well, because it's my favourite.

Friday, June 23:

It's always pretty quiet the day before a match. I have a bit of a lie-in and then there's the captain's run at the match stadium about noon. It's usually a fairly brief run-through of moves and when it ends, most players do their own thing. The forwards might do a few more lineouts, inside backs might do some more passing. I do some more kicking. Back to the hotel and rest, trying to refresh for the game. Dinner at the hotel.

Saturday, June 24:
Match day.

I have a bit of a sleep-in and go to breakfast about 9.30. About 11, a few of us go for a walk and a coffee and then back to the hotel for lunch. At 3.30, the backs and the forwards meet

Opposite page: The pre-match lineup before the test in Buenos Aires, my first venture in Argentina.
Overleaf: Ducking past a defender and about to score a crucial try against the Pumas.

separately. We walk through our moves, toss a ball about. Then it's back to the room for a while and then some of us go for a bit of a walk around the block. It's an 8.40 p.m. kickoff so that's pretty late and it makes for a long day. We have the pre-match meal at the hotel and after that I usually like to sleep for a while. I manage about an hour. Dress for going to the stadium then the last team meeting at 7 p.m. before boarding the bus. Graham Henry says a few words and we file on to the bus. Then it's the usual routine at the ground, warmups and into the match.

The weather has been good all week but it pours during the Saturday and it rains lightly during the game, making for tough conditions. The Pumas put us under a lot of pressure and the crowd is very vocal. It's a good hard-fought win and, though a win, there's no celebrating in the dressing room. It's fairly quiet because we know we didn't play to the standards we'd set ourselves, and that's partly to the credit of the Pumas.

Both teams go to an after-match function where the hit speech of the night is from our captain, Jerry Collins. His entire speech — and it wasn't an especially short one — is in Spanish, which greatly surprises and impresses our hosts. It surprises and impresses us too! We go back to the hotel for a team get-together and a bit of a singalong with Neemia Tialata on the guitar.

Sunday, June 25:
We have a recovery session in the pool in the morning then out to a restaurant for lunch. Back at the hotel, we're told the Tri-nations squad and then have dinner and leave for the airport. Our flight leaves at 1 a.m. and this time I'm able to sleep for about 10 hours. We arrive in Auckland at 5.30 a.m., head for the domestic terminal and home to Christchurch — then it's soon time to prepare for the first of the Tri-nations tests, against Australia.

Above: Getting a pass away under pressure against Argentina. Anton Oliver keeps a watchful eye on proceedings.
Opposite page: There's nothing better than that winning feeling — celebrating in Buenos Aires.

Under the Spotlight

There's much more to being a professional rugby player than just training and playing. The commercial and entertainment world in which modern rugby operates involves the players in a wide range of commercial commitments. Some are for the teams, in my case Canterbury, the Crusaders or the All Blacks, and they are mainly doing advertisements for team sponsors, and then there are individual commercial opportunities as well.

As with most things in topline rugby, I was pretty green when I arrived on the scene. All I was there for was to train and play and I didn't know anything about the extra bits. The first non-rugby activity in which I was involved was a poster shoot for the Canterbury team in my first year in the Air New Zealand NPC, in 2002. It was all completely new to me — getting dressed up in rugby gear and following the instructions of a photographer who, like all photographers, wanted that extra shot just in case. It was one of those standard poster shoots — you know, players standing looking grimly determined in front of a suitable moody background that was added later thanks to the wonders of computer technology.

Team photo shoots can be a lot of fun though because there's a lot of joking going on and there's always at least one player who will poke out his tongue or close his eyes at the wrong moment.

The whole thing took about two hours which, judging by what I know now, wasn't very long at all, but it seemed a while at the time. Team photo shoots can be a lot of fun, though, because there's a lot of joking going on and there's always at least one player who will poke out his tongue or close his eyes at the wrong moment.

The first individual promotion I did was with the Auckland halfback, Steve Devine, in my first year of Super 12, in 2003. We'd been contracted to do a television commercial, aimed at kids, promoting Vortex — those toys for throwing that are shaped like rugby balls with a tail and fin. The people doing it offered Steve and I what seemed at the time to be a bucketload of money, especially considering that very few people outside of Canterbury would have known who I was, and we thought this commercial business was for us. We spent pretty much a whole day doing it and I still cringe when I think about it. It was all very cheesy and over the top. We had a lot of fun doing it though and, while we didn't know what the finished product would look like, we just did what we were told and hoped it would turn out OK. I still haven't seen it but people who have, have told me what it's like and I'm glad I haven't.

A repetitive part of the modern player's life — signing. Tana Umaga and I oblige.

Question time. Fronting up to the news media, this time after the second test against the Lions in 2005.

It was only later in 2003 when I was first chosen for the All Blacks that I realised the full extent of the commercial obligations rugby players have. It was my first real taste of the commercial world. We spent almost a week on a series of commercial activities including billboards, posters, television commercials and other bits and pieces. It sounds a bit glamorous, and a bit like light relief from the physical side of rugby as well, but it's demanding, draining work.

Blackout! I got a full paint job as part of a promotion before the 2003 World Cup.

Some players, especially in the earlier years of the transition from amateur to professional rugby, thought the commercial work was a burden they could do without; but players these days accept it as part and parcel of their job. I know I do. We all realise how important these things are for sponsors — they invest a lot of money in rugby and in exchange for that support, we have to do our bit by being involved in the various ways they publicise their role in rugby. It's a fair quid pro quo and players know that without the sponsors, the game wouldn't be the same and certainly the opportunities for All Blacks wouldn't be the same. Some of the commercial work is incredibly creative and it's fascinating to be a part of it — players are learning things they never thought they'd know anything about. It's almost like being on a movie set at times.

It's important for us as players to go into it all with a good attitude, do the best we can and enjoy it, knowing all along that it's in our interests as well as in the wider interests of rugby.

Most professional players have an agent who organises contracts and looks after all the myriad things in which a player gets involved. My ideal agent is one who leaves the player to do the playing — and looks after most other things. I had my first meeting with an agent in 2002 during the NPC and I was pretty hesitant. It was a pretty natural reaction, I suppose. All my life, what I did and how I did it was controlled either by my parents or by me and then along came someone who said they'd take over. Of course anyone would be hesitant. I'd seen Jerry Maguire a few times — I knew what sports agents were like. Or at least, I knew how Hollywood portrayed them.

The relationship I formed with Lou Thompson of Global Sports Management — GSM — was relaxed from the start, and it's continued in that way with Dean Hegan and Warren Alcock of GSM. They didn't make me sign anything or promise a percentage of this or a percentage of that. They just said they'd look after me and Warren would become involved to tidy up the legal bits like contracts and other agreements. That's the way it's continued. They're a great bunch to work with, they never commit me to anything without having discussed it with me first and they're as protective of me as any parents would be.

Pacific Brands, a Christchurch-based company that owns the Jockey brand in New Zealand, wanted me to front a new advertising campaign. I wasn't keen at all from the start.

I'm just a shy country boy and I don't seek publicity and parading my body dressed just in undies didn't sound like a good idea. It just wasn't me.

So it was a big 'No!' from me from the start, but the GSM boys just talked me through it and then I had more discussions with the Jockey people and I gradually changed my mind. The bottom line, I suppose, was that the ads had to be tasteful and on that we were all agreed. It also sounded like fun — and it was — and I thought that it might open up other opportunities.

The deal was agreed and we went ahead and did the photo shoots. What was good for me was that I was always involved in the process of selecting which photos to use and which to reject. I wouldn't say I had the final say but I was able to state my preferences and everything that was used had my approval.

Naturally, I got a fair bit of stick from team-mates and I expected that. But it was all good-natured and they soon quietened down when I slipped them a few pairs of Jockeys.

Of course I had the advantage, when the ads finally appeared, of being involved in the process right from the start so nothing came as a surprise to me. That wasn't the case for other people. My mother, sister and girlfriend weren't at all keen, and a few friends had a similar view. Their views gradually changed, though, as the ads developed and they saw what I knew, that everything was proper and above board.

Naturally, I got a fair bit of stick from team-mates and I expected that. But it was all good-natured and they soon quietened down when I slipped them a few pairs of Jockeys. There wasn't any negative feedback.

While I was content with the way the whole thing worked, and was gratified that the reaction wasn't critical, I must admit to some embarrassment at seeing King Kong-size photos of me in undies. There was one big billboard in Durham Street in Christchurch and, once having seen it, I took great care not to drive past there again while it was still up.

Opposite page: My most talked about promotion . . .

I'm pretty lucky that I also have a personal relationship with the sportswear manufacturer, adidas, and it's a happy conjunction that adidas is also a major sponsor of the New Zealand Rugby Union and of the All Blacks. Adidas for the past few years have been great for New Zealand rugby — and of great benefit to me too.

I was fortunate enough to get to their headquarters in Germany and I met a lot of the staff, including the chairman and chief executive, Herbert Hainer, and it was great to learn that while their main role is to produce top quality product and sell as much of it as they can, they are also genuine sports enthusiasts and are great admirers of the All Blacks. I do what I can for them and I specifically promote their eyewear.

They launched a new version of the Predator boot at the start of this year and it's very technically advanced and a fantastic boot to play in. I'm not paid to say this, by the way. It really is a good boot and one of the reasons that it is so good is that their designers listen to

The adidas Predator boots that I wear — and swear by.

Promotions are not all hard work. Me and Rico Gear on the back of a Mustang during a Ford commercial shoot. In the front are netballers Irene van Dyk and Adine Wilson (driver).

Some of the All Blacks had a day out with Ford at Pukekohe before an Australian test last year: Richie McCaw, Aaron Mauger, me, Jonno Gibbes, Carl Hayman.

the views of players — we say what we'd like in a boot and they go away and produce one. What could be better than that?

Unfortunately, I haven't reached the high status of Jonah Lomu and been invited to various places around the world to do commercials or made guest appearances with stars from other sports. Jonah rubbed shoulders with Anna Kournikova so perhaps one day I might get into that league. Impossible is nothing, so goes the adidas saying.

After the European tour in 2004, a group of us played Bullrush on a ground in London against a few of the Lions for a television commercial for adidas, which sponsored both teams. It was a lot of fun. There was a bit of talk about smashing them, or them smashing us, and the television director tried to get us to look fierce but it didn't quite work because

The commercialism of rugby is something that I have grown into and have come to enjoy. It's all part of being a footballer.

the fun aspect got in the way. When we'd played our 'game', there were a few photos of mock match-ups, me against Stephen Jones and Jonny Wilkinson, for example. While it was a commercial obligation and therefore work, it was a good way to relax and let our hair down after playing rugby all year.

The commercialism of rugby is something that I have grown into and have come to enjoy. It's all part of being a footballer. Sometimes there's a commercial or a photo shoot you have to do because it's a team obligation and while it could be seen as a bit of a drag, the attitude should be just to get out there and do it and enjoy it and everyone will benefit. Get on with the job and do it. The end result in most cases — practically all cases — makes it worthwhile.

It is possible to get too caught up in the commercial side of things so it's important to remind yourself that rugby has to remain the No 1 focus, though personally I've never had any trouble knowing my priorities. It's pretty obvious that it's your ability and standing as a rugby player that creates the commercial opportunities; so if your rugby suffers, the opportunities will quite rightly dwindle.

All Blacks and Lions got together in London in 2004 to shoot an adidas commercial. Me with Jonny Wilkinson (above) and with Wilkinson and Stephen Jones (below).

I want to be known, or remembered, as a rugby player, not as someone who took commercial opportunities. GSM and I agree that commercials will be done if they're of interest and of benefit, not just for the sake of doing them and making money.

The Lions tour raised my profile and made me better known, perhaps because I had a good couple of tests, but also because the television audience for the series was so massive. This in itself created more opportunities but, again, I needed no reminding that rugby was my main priority. Everything else is secondary.

I'm often asked what I will do after rugby and it's an important consideration, because you're an ex-player for a long time. Not surprisingly at my age, it's not something I think about a lot but I have considered it. I've probably got about 10 years maximum as a rugby player, and a lot can happen in that time. I'd like to be able to set myself up in something that interests me but I don't really know what. Every player needs a life outside of rugby and that's something I'd like to develop while I'm still playing — maybe own my own business; just something to give me an interest outside of rugby, somewhere I can call in and check up on things and think of something that has nothing to do with the game I live for and love.

Above: Getting in a spot of rugby coaching — Rippa Rugby, that is.
Opposite page: Modelling the latest adidas United Training Football apparel, launched in July 2006.

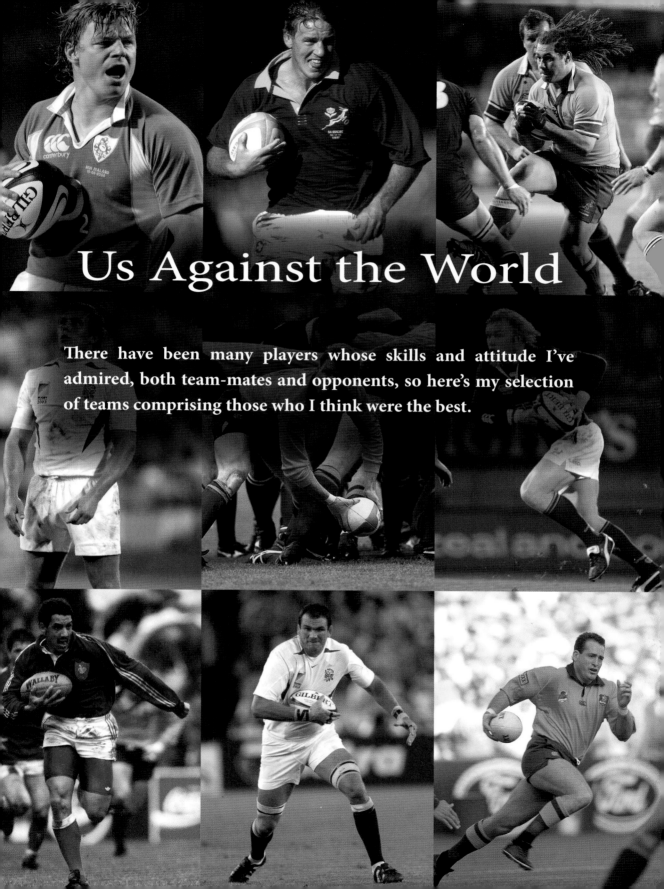

Us Against the World

There have been many players whose skills and attitude I've admired, both team-mates and opponents, so here's my selection of teams comprising those who I think were the best.

NEW ZEALAND

Fullback

Christian Cullen

I wonder sometimes if New Zealanders really appreciated how good he was. At his best, he was easily the best fullback in the world — his pace and the lines he ran made him a very difficult man to stop and if he didn't score himself, he was well capable of putting someone else in a position to do so. He was the complete attacking fullback. There was nothing wrong with his defence either.

Right wing
Joe Rokocoko

He's a friend and a team-mate, but he's also one of those players any team would love to have. He's got speed to burn, but he's also got all the skills that complement that speed and when he's got the ball in hand and the tryline near — or even not so near — you'd back him to score before you'd back the opposition to stop him. That try he scored against Wales in 2004 to ensure the win has to have been among the best tries scored in test history. I'm sorry for Jeff Wilson because he was a superlative player but Joe just eases him out. I haven't picked reserves but if I did, Jeff would be the first because he was versatile and could also kick goals.

Left wing
Jonah Lomu

Could there have been any other choice? When you're talking about the great wings of rugby, there are any number of names which could be thrown up — and then there's Jonah. He is not judged by the yardsticks which apply to everyone else. He was a phenomenon, call him what you like. He did things on the rugby field that no other player could do and he petrified the opposition. I'm sure teams spent more time working out how to stop him than they did on their own gameplans. At his peak, say in 1995 and 1996, he was far and away the dominant rugby player in the world. Give him the ball and your troubles were over. There's been no one else in the game like Jonah.

Centre
Frank Bunce

He'd been long gone from the scene when I arrived but I clearly remember seeing him on television and admiring the skills he brought to the game. He was the ideal centre, the linkman between the inside and outside backs and almost faultless in his decision-making. He knew when to pass, who to pass to, or when to make a break or take the tackle. He wasn't a star player but he was as close to indispensable as a rugby player can get. He enhanced the standards set by earlier great centres. He was a very strong defender too.

Second five-eighth
Tana Umaga

The word mana might have been invented just for him. I know he started his All Blacks life as a wing, then went to centre and ended it at second five-eighth and people will have their different opinions of where he was best suited. I don't care. I just want him in my team. He was a great team man and I know he'll be missed in the All Blacks. Younger guys looked up to him because he had the commitment and passion that epitomised the All Blacks. He was a very clever player too, always seeming to know when to do the right thing and how to be in the right place at the right time. There are plenty of opponents, too, who thought they could take him on and then got a quick lesson about defence.

First five-eighth
Andrew Mehrtens

I suppose this is the position I know most about now and so maybe in making the decision I was more ruthless. Even so, the best I've seen and the best I've played with was Mehrtens. I was fortunate enough to play outside him for Canterbury, the Crusaders and the All Blacks so I was able to admire his skills from close range. It's fair to say that a lot of what I know I learnt from him. After Grant Fox, some New Zealanders wondered whether there would ever be anyone else as dominant as him. Then along came 'Mehrts'. He could read a game like no one else, he knew instinctively where to be on the field and what to do and he so rarely made a mistake. There were times in games when things weren't going all that well and the simple remedy was so say, 'Get the ball to Mehrts, he'll sort it out'. And he usually did. I can't speak too highly of him. He was a superb team man and when I came along, and was perhaps seen as a threat, he couldn't have been more helpful.

Halfback
Graeme Bachop

I suppose this might be the surprise selection. People would expect me to put Justin Marshall here, since he and I played together and he was such a great player for the All Blacks for such a long time. But from an early age, I admired the no-nonsense way Bachop got on with the game and he had all the skills demanded of a halfback. You could never say passing was his strength, or running or kicking were his strengths — he had them all. He was superb at providing quick service to give his backs time and space.

No 8
Zinzan Brooke

He was such a skilful, versatile player. 'Zinny' also hated losing, positively loathed it, and he would do everything in his power to avoid it. And he had a lot in his power. Although I have him at No 8, he played in all three loose forward positions for New Zealand and he was adept and skilful in each. Whether it was in the tight or in the loose, Brooke was always there. I must admit to a sneaking admiration for his dropkicking style too!

Openside flanker
Richie McCaw

No surprise here, surely. The No 7 is one of the positions in which New Zealand has had riches over the years, among them the great Michael Jones and the first Grand Slam captain, Graham Mourie. Richie deserves to be mentioned in the same breath as the best. He's one of those rare players who, in a team game, can make such a huge difference through his individual efforts. In such a complex area of the game as the tackle ball, he is a master and I'm sure he outthinks the referees sometimes as well as the opposition. He is a master at snaffling the ball back and he's a superb defender. He's not a bad runner with the ball either. Any team with him in it has riches indeed.

Blindside flanker
Michael Jones

How could a team of the best New Zealanders of the past few years — or of any era really — not include Michael Jones? They called him the Ice Man and I was never sure it was because he didn't have any nerves or because he had so many injuries he always seemed to have ice on him somewhere. I wished I'd been able to play in the same sides as him. He began his test life as an openside flanker, being one of the stars of the World Cup win in 1987, and continued for more than a decade, playing in the three loose forward positions and being outstanding in whatever he did. His handling was superb, his defence immense. And to think he achieved everything he did despite that horrific knee injury in 1989 and despite missing so much rugby because he wouldn't compromise his principles and play on Sundays.

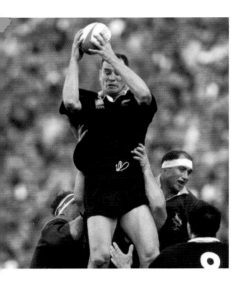

Locks

Robin Brooke

Robin wasn't a flashy player — he just got on and did what was required of him and did it well and never let up. He was especially valuable in his main tasks of taking ball in lineouts and from kickoffs. He also, and I suspect it's not politically correct to say this these days, was a hard man in the old rugby sense — in the phrase players use, he would never take a backward step. Such attitudes may be frowned on by people off the field, but people on the field know that they're a distinct advantage.

Chris Jack

He has a huge impact on every game he plays because of the amount of work he puts in. From the age of 20, it was obvious he was going to be a long-term fixture in the All Blacks, barring injury, and so it's proved to be. He's been one of the mainstays of all the teams with which I've been involved and there's a nice feeling of security when he's up ahead of you doing the hard work. But it's not just grunt work he does. He gets around the field like a back and some of you may recall some of the deft little kicks he's put through from time to time. He's another ideal team man.

Tighthead prop
Olo Brown

He was another player well finished by the time I came on the scene, but I can remember watching him and hearing plenty of talk about him. It's only other front row forwards who truly understand front row play, but I do know the value of a scrum that stays rock-solid and that's generally what they did when Olo was in the team.

Loosehead prop
Carl Hayman

I know, I know, he's a specialist tighthead — but I'm a back after all, so what am I supposed to know? But how could I pick a team without 'Zarga', the strong man of All Blacks rugby? I happen to know that he has played at loosehead and Hayman being Hayman, he'd probably play at halfback just to get in a team. He's another of those unsung front row guys who just get on with the job, rarely speak or get upset with things, but you get this great feeling of security when you're playing behind them. He has the respect of team-mates and opponents alike and he's another great man to have around in the team.

Hooker

Sean Fitzpatrick (captain)

Could there be anyone else? He played so long for New Zealand he seemed to see off a generation or two of other hookers and he and the All Blacks were as one. If there were a grand final for competitiveness, he and Zinzan Brooke would be in it. One of the things I admired about Fitzpatrick was that he worked hard at his game and never took anything for granted. He was also a great leader for New Zealand, daring everyone to follow him. I think the only people who would have been relieved when injury forced Fitzpatrick's retirement would have been opponents and referees.

So that's my New Zealand lineup and, I'm sure you'll agree it's pretty formidable. I apologise to all the great players I haven't chosen but, well, I can only squeeze 15 into a team, just like a real selector.

Now for the opponents and, again, it's people I've seen play, even if only on television.

WORLD XV

Fullback
Serge Blanco (France)

This may seem a bit of a strange choice because he comes from another era entirely when the game was quite different. But I think that almost alone he ushered in the era of the modern fullback, one who saw himself as the first line of attack rather than the last line of defence. I know he had a terrifically long career — he first played against the All Blacks in 1977 — but he never seemed to lose form or influence. I used to love watching his loping running style and how he'd get to places opponents could never have thought he'd reach.

Right wing
David Campese (Australia)

Campese could be brilliant, was one of those invaluable players who could do something utterly unexpected that could change a game. His skills were superb — remember that try he scored against the All Blacks in the World Cup semi-final in Dublin in 1991? I've seen it since on video and I doubt many other players could have brought that off. As long as he was fit, Australia could never leave him out, whether he was on the wing or at fullback. He was one of those players who graced the game and whose value may not have been fully appreciated until he was gone.

Left wing
Lote Tuqiri (Australia)

This may seem a bit of a strange choice because he hasn't been playing rugby for all that long — for less time than me in fact! He's got huge talent, though, and I know he's a marked man whenever New Zealand teams are against him. It's just that he's such a strong, powerful runner with the ball and a very difficult man to stop. Like a lot of former league players, he knows instinctively how to run lines well and, like most Australians, he's great with the ball in the air.

Centre
Brian O'Driscoll (Ireland)

It was unfortunate that New Zealanders didn't see much of him with the Lions in 2005. He's a very fine player — like the best of centres, he makes the right decisions at the right times and when he decides to go on his own, he can be a difficult man to stop. He's got strength, speed and a respectable sidestep.

Second five-eighth
Jeremy Guscott (England)

They don't call the positions centre and second-five in Britain — that's a purely New Zealand habit. The British and Irish teams play the two-centre game, which is slightly different from what we do. Guscott was a great servant of England and Lions rugby and I don't think New Zealanders generally appreciate how good he was. Like all good midfielders, he was strong on defence despite his relatively slight build, but perhaps his greatest strength was his ability on attack. He seemed to need just the sniff of a chance of a break and he was off and his speed and agility made him a difficult man to pin down.

First five-eighth
Jonny Wilkinson (England)

The position is flyhalf in England, standoff or out-half in other places, but we know what it is. We also know how good Jonny Wilkinson is, and not just because he dropkicked the goal that won England the World Cup in 2003. Clive Woodward would have done anything to get Wilkinson into his teams, and for good reason. He's a very complete rugby player, much more than just the kicking first-five he's often accused of being. He reads a game well, he runs well, he's got all the skills, and he's never been noted for failing on defence. Fully fit, he's probably the best first-five England has ever had.

Halfback
Nick Farr-Jones (Australia)

You probably thought George Gregan had been playing for Australia for so long that you'd forgotten there were other halfbacks before him. Well, as good as George has been, Nick Farr-Jones is my choice. I always admired him when I was a youngster because he seemed always to have unflappable control behind the scrum and always seemed to somehow gain enough time to do what he had to do. He never seemed rushed or panicked. He had a terrific pass, could kick well, and he was also a good running halfback — all the qualities a good halfback needs. He was the captain as well. He was crucial to the Wallabies' World Cup win in 1991.

No 8
Gary Teichmann (South Africa)

Through the mid to late-90s, he was one of the leading forwards in the world and he always seemed a handful when playing against New Zealand teams. South African forwards are known for their bulk and competitiveness rather than their skill, which is a bit unfair on some of them. Teichmann was one of those players who had the skill as well as a fierce commitment. I never played against him, but I'm sure those who did would have respected him for his ability and for what he was capable of. He was the Springboks' captain for 36 of his 42 tests and that says a lot for his value.

Openside flanker
George Smith (Australia)

He's probably not Justin Marshall's greatest mate, but he's a fine player as anyone who has ever played against him, or even just seen him play, would acknowledge. He's the classic Aussie 'breakaway' — into everything all day, never ceasing to try to win the ball for his team and never ceasing to be a thorn in the side of his opponents. Like any good openside, and he's among the best, he tests the laws to their limits and it sometimes seems, as with Richie McCaw, that he knows more about the tackle ball law than referees do. Smith is one of those players I'd love to be in the same team as some time.

Blindside flanker
Schalk Burger (South Africa)

I don't particularly enjoy him coming at me in matches nor do I especially admire him pointing at me from the back of the lineout, but I happily admit he's a fine player. It's easy to forget how young he is and that he's only been playing at the top level since 2004. He's a big man but very fit and very fast and he's got an all-action game. He seems to pop up all over the field, throwing his body round. He's the ideal South African flanker — big enough to combat the size of the forwards they produce but fit enough and fast enough to make a huge difference in the loose.

Locks
John Eales (Australia)

Was there anything this man could not do? He was among the best lineout forwards in the world, if not the best; he was one of the strengths of the Australian pack; he was a great captain and when there was no one else to do the job, he'd kick the goals as well. Then he'd make the after-match speeches. Is there anyone in New Zealand watching that day in Wellington who will ever forget him nonchalantly kicking the last-minute goal to win the test? As New Zealanders, we were gutted; but as New Zealanders, we admired the complete allround rugby player.

Martin Johnson (England) (captain)

John Hart knew something when he plucked the gangly youth called Martin Johnson out of the King Country and put him in his New Zealand Colts side. The only problem was that Johnson was English and was returning to England. Pity. He was the dominant forward in the world in his day and for England and the Lions, an inspirational captain. I've no doubt he was a key factor in England winning the World Cup in 2003 and I'm sure he would have made a difference with the Lions in 2005. He was hard and uncompromising on the field — precisely what you want.

Tighthead prop
Os du Randt (South Africa)

His build is impressive and his fitness and attitude even more so. I've had the pleasure — if that's the right word — of playing against him and can see from close up just what an asset he is to his teams. He may be getting long in the tooth for a rugby player, but I bet his teams would rather have him than not. He is one of the last still playing from the South African side that beat the All Blacks in the World Cup final in 1995.

Loosehead prop
Ollie Le Roux (South Africa)

If I'd said Andre-Henri Le Roux, you wouldn't have known who I was talking about. But surely everyone knows of Ollie Le Roux, the genial giant who played for the Sharks before moving to the Cheetahs. He's one of the great characters of world rugby and also one of the great veterans, having been around since the start of the Super 12. He's technically a very good prop — so I'm told — and brings to the field an infectious enthusiasm. He spent a lot of time on the bench for South Africa so maybe that's why he's all energy when he gets on the field.

Hooker
Phil Kearns (Australia)

I never played against Phil Kearns but he's still a very well-known figure in the game, probably because of his television comments role. I know the All Blacks used to rate him highly and he seemed to save his competitive, annoying best for when he was playing for Australia against New Zealand. I'm told he and Sean Fitzpatrick used to snarl away at each other in the tight stuff, so perhaps it's just as well my teams don't actually play. From my observations, guys like Kearns and John Eales made all the difference to Australian forward play in the 1990s.

So that's my two teams. It was a lot of fun picking them, especially knowing my selections would never be tested. My two captains, I thought, were obvious. No one could go past Sean Fitzpatrick as the All Blacks captain, but the choice for the World team was a little harder. John Eales was a fine leader for the Wallabies, but I think I gave the job to Martin Johnson because of his wider leadership roles with Leicester, England and the Lions.

Statistics

Daniel Carter first-class record (to 31 July, 2006)

Number	Date	Team	Opponent	Venue
1	18.7.2002	Canterbury	Marlborough	Blenheim
2	24.7.2002	Canterbury	Mid Canterbury	Ashburton
3	9.8.2002	Canterbury	East Coast	Christchurch
4	16.8.2002	Canterbury	Wellington	Wellington
5	25.8.2002	Canterbury	Bay of Plenty	Rotorua
6	13.9.2002	Canterbury	Northland	Christchurch
7	28.9.2002	Canterbury	North Harbour	Christchurch
8	5.10.2002	Canterbury	Taranaki	New Plymouth
9	18.10.2002	Canterbury	Auckland	Christchurch
10	22.2.2003	Crusaders	Hurricanes	Christchurch
11	1.3.2003	Crusaders	Reds	Christchurch
12	8.3.2003	Crusaders	Blues	Albany
13	14.3.2003	Crusaders	Chiefs	Christchurch
14	29.3.2003	Crusaders	Highlanders	Dunedin
15	5.4.2003	Crusaders	Waratahs	Sydney
16	12.4.2003	Crusaders	Cats	Christchurch
17	18.4.2003	Crusaders	Sharks	Christchurch
18	26.4.2003	Crusaders	Bulls	Pretoria
19	3.5.2003	Crusaders	Stormers	Cape Town
20	9.5.2003	Crusaders	Brumbies	Canberra
21	16.5.2003	Crusaders	Hurricanes	Christchurch
22	24.5.2003	Crusaders	Blues	Auckland
23	21.6.2003	New Zealand	Wales	Hamilton
24	28.6.2003	New Zealand	France	Christchurch
25	26.7.2003	New Zealand	Australia	Sydney
26	11.10.2003	New Zealand	Italy	Melbourne
27	17.10.2003	New Zealand	Canada	Melbourne
28	24.10.2003	New Zealand	Tonga	Brisbane
29	8.11.2003	New Zealand	South Africa	Melbourne
30	20.11.2003	New Zealand	France	Sydney
31	21.2.2004	Crusaders	Waratahs	Christchurch
32	27.2.2004	Crusaders	Blues	Christchurch
33	6.3.2004	Crusaders	Reds	Brisbane
34	20.3.2004	Crusaders	Chiefs	Hamilton

Status	Position	T	C	P	DG	Totals
RS	substitute	1				5
RS	2nd five-eighth	2				10
RS	2nd five-eighth	3				15
NPC	2nd five-eighth					
NPC	1st five-eighth					
NPC, RS	1st five-eighth	1				5
NPC, RS	substitute					
NPC	1st five-eighth					
NPC sf	substitute					
S12	1st five-eighth	2				10
S12	2nd five-eighth			3		9
S12	1st five-eighth					
S12	1st five-eighth		2	4		16
S12	1st five-eighth	1	2	1		12
S12	1st five-eighth					
S12	1st five-eighth					
S12	1st five-eighth			1		3
S12	2nd five-eighth					
S12	2nd five-eighth		6	2		18
S12	2nd five-eighth		2	2	1	13
S12 sf	2nd five-eighth		3	5		21
S12 f	2nd five-eighth					
test	2nd five-eighth	1	6	1		20
test	2nd five-eighth		2	4		16
TN	substitute	1	1			7
RWC	2nd five-eighth	1	6			17
RWC	2nd five-eighth		9			18
RWC	2nd five-eighth	1				5
RWC qf	substitute					
RWC po	substitute		4			8
S12	2nd five-eighth		1	4		14
S12	2nd five-eighth	1	1	4		19
S12	2nd five-eighth			5		15
S12	2nd five-eighth		2	4		16

Number	Date	Team	Opponent	Venue
35	27.3.2004	Crusaders	Highlanders	Christchurch
36	3.4.2004	Crusaders	Brumbies	Christchurch
37	17.4.2004	Crusaders	Cats	Johannesburg
38	24.4.2004	Crusaders	Bulls	Christchurch
39	1.5.2004	Crusaders	Stormers	Christchurch
40	7.5.2004	Crusaders	Hurricanes	Wellington
41	15.5.2004	Crusaders	Stormers	Christchurch
42	22.5.2004	Crusaders	Brumbies	Canberra
43	1.6.2004	Probables	Possibles	Auckland
44	12.6.2004	New Zealand	England	Dunedin
45	19.6.2004	New Zealand	England	Auckland
46	10.7.2004	New Zealand	Pacific Islands	Albany
47	17.7.2004	New Zealand	Australia	Wellington
48	24.7.2004	New Zealand	South Africa	Christchurch
49	7.8.2004	New Zealand	Australia	Sydney
50	5.9.2004	Canterbury	Bay of Plenty	Mt Maunganui
51	12.9.2004	Canterbury	Taranaki	New Plymouth
52	18.9.2004	Canterbury	Southland	Christchurch
53	24.9.2004	Canterbury	Waikato	Hamilton
54	2.10.2004	Canterbury	Auckland	Auckland
55	9.10.2004	Canterbury	Northland	Christchurch
56	16.10.2004	Canterbury	Bay of Plenty	Christchurch
57	23.10.2004	Canterbury	Wellington	Wellington
58	13.11.2004	New Zealand	Italy	Rome
59	20.11.2004	New Zealand	Wales	Cardiff
60	27.11.2004	New Zealand	France	Paris
61	26.2.2005	Crusaders	Brumbies	Canberra
62	5.3.2005	Crusaders	Chiefs	Christchurch
63	12.3.2005	Crusaders	Reds	Nelson
64	19.3.2005	Crusaders	Blues	Auckland
65	2.4.2005	Crusaders	Waratahs	Sydney
66	9.4.2005	Crusaders	Bulls	Pretoria
67	16.4.2005	Crusaders	Stormers	Cape Town
68	23.4.2005	Crusaders	Cats	Christchurch

Status	Position	T	C	P	DG	Totals
S12	2nd five-eighth		5	2		16
S12	2nd five-eighth		4	4		20
S12	2nd five-eighth	2	4	2		24
S12	2nd five-eighth		4	4		20
S12	2nd five-eighth	1	1	4		19
S12	2nd five-eighth	1		1		8
S12 sf	2nd five-eighth		1	5		17
S12 f	2nd five-eighth	1	4			13
NZ trial	2nd five-eighth		3	1		9
test	2nd five-eighth		3	5		21
test	2nd five-eighth	1	4	1		16
test	2nd five-eighth		4	1		11
TN	2nd five-eighth		1	3		11
TN	2nd five-eighth			5		15
TN	2nd five-eighth			4		12
NPC, RS	centre					
NPC	centre		2	3		13
NPC, RS	fullback		4	1		11
NPC	fullback		3	3		15
NPC	2nd five-eighth		2	3		13
NPC, RS	2nd five-eighth	1	9			23
NPC sf	fullback		5	3		19
NPC f	fullback		4	4		20
test	1st five-eighth	1	7			19
test	1st five-eighth		1	3		11
test	1st five-eighth	1	4	4		25
S12	fullback			2		6
S12	1st five-eighth	1	6	1		20
S12	1st five-eighth	1	4	3		22
S12	1st five-eighth		4	1		11
S12	2nd five-eighth		2	3		13
S12	1st five-eighth			5		15
S12	1st five-eighth	1	3	2		17
S12	substitute		1			2

Number	Date	Team	Opponent	Venue
69	29.4.2005	Crusaders	Sharks	Christchurch
70	7.5.2005	Crusaders	Highlanders	Dunedin
71	20.5.2005	Crusaders	Hurricanes	Christchurch
72	28.5.2005	Crusaders	Waratahs	Christchurch
73	10.6.2005	New Zealand	Fiji	Albany
74	24.6.2005	New Zealand	British Isles	Christchurch
75	2.7.2005	New Zealand	British Isles	Wellington
76	30.7.2005	New Zealand	South Africa	Cape Town
77	13.8.2005	New Zealand	Australia	Sydney
78	8.10.2005	Canterbury	Auckland	Christchurch
79	14.10.2005	Canterbury	Otago	Christchurch
80	5.11.2005	New Zealand	Wales	Cardiff
81	19.11.2005	New Zealand	England	London
82	11.2.2006	Crusaders	Highlanders	Christchurch
83	18.2.2006	Crusaders	Reds	Brisbane
84	25.2.2006	Crusaders	Sharks	Timaru
85	4.3.2006	Crusaders	Blues	Christchurch
86	10.3.2006	Crusaders	Chiefs	Hamilton
87	17.3.2006	Crusaders	Cats	Christchurch
88	1.4.2006	Crusaders	Hurricanes	Wellington
89	7.4.2006	Crusaders	Waratahs	Christchurch
90	15.4.2006	Crusaders	Cheetahs	Christchurch
91	21.4.2006	Crusaders	Force	Perth
92	29.4.2006	Crusaders	Stormers	Cape Town
93	5.5.2006	Crusaders	Bulls	Pretoria
94	12.5.2006	Crusaders	Brumbies	Christchurch
95	20.5.2006	Crusaders	Bulls	Christchurch
96	27.5.2006	Crusaders	Hurricanes	Christchurch
97	24.6.2006	New Zealand	Argentina	Buenos Aires
98	8.7.2006	New Zealand	Australia	Christchurch
99	22.7.2006	New Zealand	South Africa	Wellington
100	29.7.2006	New Zealand	Australia	Brisbane

Status	Position	T	C	P	DG	Totals
S12	1st five-eighth	1	7			19
S12	1st five-eighth		3	2		12
S12 sf	1st five-eighth	1	4	3		22
S12 f	1st five-eighth		3	2		12
test	1st five-eighth	1	5			15
test	1st five-eighth		1	3		11
test	1st five-eighth	2	4	5		33
TN	1st five-eighth		1	3		11
TN	1st five-eighth		2	3		13
NPC, RS	1st five-eighth		1	1		5
NPC sf	1st five-eighth		2	1		7
test	1st five-eighth	2	5	2		26
test	1st five-eighth		2	3		13
S14	1st five-eighth		3	4		18
S14	1st five-eighth	2	4	3		27
S14	1st five-eighth			3	1	12
S14	1st five-eighth		2	6		22
S14	1st five-eighth	1	2	2		15
S14	1st five-eighth		5	1		13
S14	1st five-eighth		2	2		10
S14	1st five-eighth		2	1		7
S14	1st five-eighth	2	6	2		28
S14	1st five-eighth		1	2		8
S14	substitute		2			4
S14	1st five-eighth		3	2	1	15
S14	1st five-eighth		3	4		18
S14 sf	1st five-eighth		2	1	1	10
S14 f	1st five-eighth		1	4		14
test	1st five-eighth	1	2	2		15
TN	1st five-eighth		3	2		12
TN	1st five-eighth		2	7		25
TN	1st five-eighth		1	1	1	8
Subtotals		40	232	200	5	
Total points		200	464	600	15	1279

Dan CARTER

Most points in all matches for New Zealand

	Matches	Points
Grant Fox	78	1067
Andrew Mehrtens	72	964
Don Clarke	89	781
Fergie McCormick	44	453
Dan Carter	**28**	**414**

Most points for New Zealand in tests

	Tests	Tries	Con	PG	DG	Total	Average
Andrew Mehrtens	70	7	169	188	10	967	13.81
Grant Fox	46	1	118	128	7	645	14.02
Dan Carter	**28**	**13**	**80**	**62**	**1**	**414**	**14.78**

Highest points scorers for New Zealand in a single test

	Opponent	Tries	Con	PG	DG	Total
Simon Culhane	Japan (1995)	1	20	-	-	45
Tony Brown	Italy (1999)	1	11	3	-	36
Dan Carter	**Lions (2005)**	**2**	**4**	**5**	**-**	**33**
Carlos Spencer	Argentina (1997)	2	10	1	-	33
Andrew Mehrtens	Ireland (1997)	1	5	6	-	33
Tony Brown	Tonga (2000)	1	12	1	-	32
Marc Ellis	Japan (1995)	6	-	-	-	30
Tony Brown	Samoa (2001)	3	3	3	-	30
Andrew Mehrtens	Australia (1999)	-	1	9	-	29
Andrew Mehrtens	France (2000)	-	1	9	-	29
Leon MacDonald	Tonga (2003)	1	12	-	-	29
Andrew Mehrtens	Canada (1995)	1	7	3	-	28
Allan Hewson	Australia (1982)	1	2	5	1	26
Grant Fox	Fiji (1987)	-	10	2	-	26
Dan Carter	**Wales (2005)**	**2**	**5**	**2**	**-**	**26**
Tony Brown	Samoa (1999)	-	7	4	-	26
Grant Fox	W. Samoa (1993)	-	2	7	-	25
Jeff Wilson	Fiji (1997)	5	-	-	-	25
Carlos Spencer	South Africa (1997)	1	4	4	-	25
Dan Carter	**France (2004)**	**1**	**4**	**4**	**-**	**25**
Dan Carter	**South Africa (2006)**	**-**	**2**	**7**	**-**	**25**

Highest All-time Test Points-scorers	Tests	Tries	Con	PG	DG	Points	Average
Neil Jenkins (Wales & British Isles)	91	11	131	248	10	1090	11.76
Diego Dominguez (Argentina & Italy)	76	9	133	214	19	1010	13.51
Andrew Mehrtens (New Zealand)	70	7	169	188	10	967	13.81
Michael Lynagh (Australia)	72	17	140	177	9	911	12.65
Matt Burke (Australia)	81	29	104	174	1	878	10.84
Jonny Wilkinson (England & British Isles)	57	6	129	181	21	864	15.16
Gavin Hastings (Scotland & British Isles)	67	18	87	160	-	733	10.94
Hugo Porta (Argentina)	66	12	91	115	28	656	9.94
Grant Fox (New Zealand)	46	1	118	128	7	645	14.02
Percy Montgomery (South Africa)	78	18	98	113	6	643	8.4
Ronan O'Gara (Ireland & British Isles)	64	9	101	121	9	637	10.0
Nicky Little (Fiji)	59	2	104	125	2	599	10.15
David Humphreys (Ireland)	72	7	88	110	8	565	7.85
Stephen Jones (Wales & British Isles)	59	6	92	99	3	520	8.81
Gareth Rees (Canada)	55	7	51	110	9	491	8.93
Gonzalo Quesada (Argentina)	37	4	68	103	7	486	13.14
Stefano Bettarello (Italy)	55	7	46	103	18	483	8.78
Chris Paterson (Scotland)	66	20	55	88	2	480	7.3
Bob Ross (Canada)	57	7	52	83	10	418	7.33
Dan Carter (New Zealand)	**28**	**13**	**80**	**62**	**1**	**414**	**14.78**
Rob Andrew (England & British Isles)	76	2	34	87	23	407	5.36